# ISSEI

# The Shadow Generation

一世

[影の世代]

*Rooted in Japanese
Values, Planted
on American Soil*

By
Tsukasa Matsueda, Ed.D.

ISSEI – The Shadow Generation © 2006 by Tsukasa Matsueda

Library of Congress Control Number: 2006936507
Data available upon request.

Cover Designer: Chisato Watanabe
Layout: David Kawakita, Kawakita Graphics
Production Assistant: Jill Shiraki
Printed by Paper & Ink, Redwood City, California

Published by Japanese Cultural and Community Center of
Northern California
1840 Sutter Street, San Francisco, California 94115
(415) 567-5505
www.jcccnc.org

ISBN: 0-9788531-0-5

## Songs Our Parents Taught Us

*Wakamono yo*, (Young ones)
   You, with your glittering eyes,
     witness life's beauty,
     its mystery and storms,
Dream your yume (dreams),
     *benkyo seyo* (study), and *gambare* (work hard)!

Fate may trample you;
     there will be constant *kurou* (struggle);
*Sore ga jinsei da* (that's life),
     but *makeruna* (don't lose)!
Make another *yume* (dream),
     *gambare* (work hard), again and again,
       and you will *katsu* (succeed)!

*Wakamono yo* (young one), you are not alone.
All the world is there to help you,
     each living thing, every speck of resources,
       the glittering sun, the beautiful moon,
         all will help you!
*Sonkei seo* (respect them), *daiji ni seyo* (treasure them),
     their generosity is *mottainai* (not to be wasted)!
And the family, the friends,
     even people you don't know...
       the farmers, the fishermen,
         the miners, the railway workers,
     they will all help you *wakamono yo* (young one).
*Minna no okage de* (with all of their help),
     you will *katsu* (succeed)!

So *minna to kyoroku seyo* (work with them),
     *benkyo seyo* (study with them),
       learn from them, and *gambare* (perservere)!
But, don't forget to *tanoshimu* (enjoy life) my young companion,
     because there is joy and beauty in life too!
As you savor all of life, give *kansha* (thanks) to all,
     say *arigato* (thanks) each day for their kindness.
Soon, it will be your turn to help, encourage,
     and lift the young and the old,
       and all the world!
So, *isshoukenmei ni* (with all your might)
     embrace life and hope!
Shape and fashion your life,
     *wakamono yo* (young ones)!

- Tsukasa Matsueda

# Table of Contents

# Table of Contents

*Issei* - The Shadow Generation

# Note on the Title

"*Issei*: the Shadow Generation" conveys two basic thoughts concerning the *Issei*. First, many people at the present time do not know much about the *Issei*. To many, the *Issei* remain a shadowy people in the past. Even those who had close and long contact with the *Issei* did not fully know and understand them because of language difficulties and cultural differences. So the word shadow (kage) describes the *Issei's* "hazy" image.

Second, the word *kage* in Japanese has more than one meaning. When the honorific *o* is prefixed to the word *kage*, as in *okage*, it can also mean "thanks to...", "owing to...", or "because of..." so that the Japanese title can be interpreted to mean, "Due to the efforts of the *Issei* generation, the *Nisei* children, in particular, became good and productive citizens."

Our hope is that the *Issei* legacy will emerge from the shadow and appear under a brighter light so that their efforts can be fully appreciated. Once better understood, the *Issei* will no longer be the "shadow generation", and in this brighter world, the *Issei* legacy can be shared by a larger community of people and possibly enhance and enrich contemporary society.

# Acknowledgements

I am enormously and deeply grateful to all the people who encouraged me to write this story of the *Issei*. Marjorie Fletcher, Florence Dobashi, and Bill Sakai of the San Francisco Bay Area *Nikkei* Singles were among the first to encourage me to talk and write about the *Issei*. Dr. Ben Kobashigawa, Associate Professor at San Francisco State University, attended one of my talks with several of his students and immediately urged me to "turn this talk into a book." Margaret Blair, a psychologist and a family counselor, who read one of the earliest drafts, said, "I've learned so much. You must get it finished as quickly as you can." I must acknowledge Dr. Joseph Yasutake, along with the many, many people who came to listen to my talks in various Northern California communities, made comments, and asked questions which encouraged me to expand and revise my original draft. Dr. Bob Suzuki, former President of California State Polytechnic University, Pomona, and Dr. Alfred Bloom, a noted Buddhist scholar who once taught at Harvard University, both took precious time from their still hectic schedules to appraise my manuscript. I thank them for their critique, their warm support, and their continuing interest and kindness. Cartoonist Jack Matsuoka and artists Chisato Watanabe and David Kawakita all added their unique and creative touches which effectively enhanced the book. Writers Sally Barlow-Perez and Wells Wadleigh served as editors for different stages of my manuscript, helped me to clarify my thoughts, and polish my writing. Thanks also to Lisa Kobayashi, super mom, who deciphered my handwriting, typed it into a more readable manuscript and cheered me on. Special thanks to Yosh Oshima, who most patiently taught me, the greatest "Computer Dummy" in the world, how to use the Japanese language setting in my computer which enabled me to add the Japanese words in the Japanese - English glossary and on the cover of the book.

With all the encouragement I received, I managed to complete the book, but needed a publisher to complete my venture. Fortunately, Paul Osaki, the Executive Director of the Japanese Cultural & Community Center of Northern California, expressed his willingness to publish my book, and somehow carved time from his frenetic schedule to do so. From the beginning, he has focused on acknowledging the *Issei* contribution to the welfare of the Japanese American community. I also must express my gratitude to Jill Shiraki whom Paul recommended to help with the final product. Her enthusiasm and her deep knowledge truly helped in crafting the writing into a polished product.

Finally, I gratefully acknowledge the support of my wife, June, who not only encouraged me to write this book, but made sure that I would have the maximum amount of "free" time from the family schedule so that I would be able to write. She was my most severe and "best" critic. Both of our children, Bob and Julie, and their spouses, Ranko and Jon, listened to and read my story and added critical suggestions. Ken, Mika, and Lee, the three grandchildren, said, "Grandpa is writing a book. That's so cool." Those words spurred me on, no doubt.

Thanks to all, I was able to write about what I consider to be the greatest legacy to us.

# Foreword
by
## Bob H. Suzuki, Ph.D.
President *Emeritus*
California State Polytechnic University, Pomona

Much has been written about the seemingly phenomenal success of the American-born Japanese, especially the *Nisei*, the second generation of Japanese in America. Their success has led some writers to refer to them as the "model minority." While this label perpetuates a stereotype and is quite overblown, no one can deny that by such socioeconomic measures as educational level and income, the Nisei have been very successful.

In comparison, very little has been written about the *Issei*, the immigrant parents of the *Nisei* and the first generation of Japanese in America. As implied in the title of this book, they have, indeed, been a "shadow generation" whose role in the success of the *Nisei* has been almost hidden in the background. Nevertheless, the *Issei* obviously had to play a hugely influential role in the upbringing of the *Nisei* and can take much of the credit for their success. Therefore, few would question that a great deal might be learned about effective parenting by examining the values, thinking and child rearing practices of the *Issei*.

Tsukasa Matsueda, has the rare ability among American-born Japanese to read, write and speak fluently in both English and Japanese. He is also well versed in both Japanese and American culture. This unique bilingual/bicultural ability has enabled him, on the one hand, to converse and interact extensively with the *Issei* and to gain deep insights into their values, customs and behavioral patterns. On the other hand, it has also enabled him to communicate and interpret this understanding of the *Issei* to American-born Japanese as well as others not literate in Japanese.

To reinforce Matsueda's assertion, it is important to document the history and legacy of the *Issei* generation not only to gain a deeper understanding of the *Issei's* values, thinking and child rearing practices, but also for the lessons they may hold for addressing some of the most pressing social problems we are facing as a society. In writing this book, Matsueda does a commendable job in meeting this objective. I hope the book receives wide readership because I believe the readers will be richly rewarded with valuable, new insights.

Bob H. Suzuki
Alhambra, California
June 2006

# **Introduction**

When I was much, much younger than I am now, I was ashamed of my parents. Let me rephrase that. I was ashamed of them when I compared them to my Caucasian friends' parents because they seemed unsophisticated and coarse in appearance and behavior. I remember when I was in high school, I did not attend the Father and Son Night because my father was a gardener and could hardly speak English. I thought that my parents were out of sync with the mainstream American community. I do not remember any of my *Nisei*[1] friends bringing their fathers to the event either. However, within the confines of my home and the Japanese community, I respected and loved them and I did not think they were "out of sync" or old fashioned.

As I grew older and shared with them the concentration camp[2] experiences, my opinion of them changed imperceptibly. I thought of the difficult times they had faced from the time they landed in the United States in the late 19th century, through the Great Depression of the 1930's, the modest life they created was taken away so unfairly and cruelly in the 1940's that it saddened and angered me at the same time. Later, after we were released from the concentration camp and had to start over from scratch, my respect for them deepened. When I became a father of two children and had to struggle to do well in my profession and be a good father at the same time, my respect and love for my parents and other *Issei* deepened. Thus, through the years, I began to realize that one of the most privileged and rewarding experiences I have had, is that I was able to live among the *Issei*, and work and talk with them for a good part of my life. One of the saddest experiences has been to see almost all of them pass from our midst.

Belatedly, I realized that these people who migrated from Japan to America, the *Issei*, were one of the rarest and finest groups of people I have ever met. However, there are many people today who do not share my opinion of the *Issei* and do not give too much thought to them and what their lives have meant to us. They do not seem to fully understand how strong, patient, and resilient the *Issei* were, as they persevered through endless suffering and difficulties.

Many of the *Nisei* seem not to understand how their own basic characters and personalities were shaped by their *Issei* parents. Unfortunately, many *Nisei* did not fully understand Japanese and could not thoroughly comprehend their parents' teachings. In turn, most of the *Issei* never learned to speak English well enough to communicate their thoughts to their children as clearly as they wanted to. Sadly, both parties could not discuss their differences or completely express their opinions or their feelings, so it was not surprising that they ended up with a fragmented and incomplete view of each other.

Presumptuous as I may be, and encouraged by those whom I mentioned earlier, I would like to describe my understanding of the *Issei*'s views on life - their thoughts and feelings mostly as they related to their children's upbringing. Because I am able to speak, read, and write in Japanese, I was able to share their experiences. Those are some of the most cherished and warmest moments in my life. Most of what I have recorded here was told to me by the *Issei* and basically, it is no more than that. I do not pretend to have taken a scientific or professional analysis. Many of the stories were related to me in regional dialects, but here, wherever I have used Japanese terms, I have changed the dialects to standard Japanese. Unfortunately, the charm and warmth found in the dialects is missing.

I will try to tell their side of the story as faithfully as I can. For most of the *Issei* whom I came to know, the single most important task in life was to do the best they could do for the sake of their children. (*kodomo no tame ni*). Most of my information was gathered from the many, many *Issei* I knew in Stockton and San Mateo, where I spent a substantial amount of my life. In addition to that, I met many more *Issei* during World War II at the Rohwer and Tule Lake Concentration Camps. After my retirement from public school teaching, spanning over a period of 33 years, I have had the privilege of meeting and helping *Issei* at *Yu-Ai Kai* (Friendship and Love Center) Japanese American Community Senior Services in San Jose, for over ten years. The quotes used throughout the book are taken from the interviews and conversations I have had with the *Issei*. The individuals are unidentified to allow the image of the *Issei* the readers may know to remain open, so that the readers may begin to draw him/her out from the shadow, and perhaps, better understand their character and influence.

The *Issei* I met were immigrants from many different parts of Japan. I had the valuable experience of talking to *Issei* who worked on farms, in the floral industry, or the fishing industry, and others who were owners of small or large businesses. I also talked to some who labored as miners or railroad workers. Additionally, I have had the privilege of talking to *Issei* from different religious background including Presbyterians, Methodists, Episcopalians, Catholics and Baptists as well as Buddhists from the *Gedatsu, Jōdo Shinshu, Higashi Honganji, Kōyasan, Zen, Nichiren,* and *Jōdo* sects. Others I spoke to were members of *Shinto, Seicho no Ie, Tenrikyō,* and *Konkokyō* churches.

All of these *Issei*, from such varied backgrounds, suffered varying degrees of racism and discrimination, but they did not permit these obstacles to determine how to carry out their dreams or raise their children. In the awesome task of rearing their children, often under unfavorable circumstances, the *Issei* wanted to instill the values that they themselves were taught. They were convinced that these values would help their *Nisei* children overcome the difficulties that life would bring.

Although the *Issei* came from such diverse backgrounds, in most cases their views on life and child rearing were remarkably similar, and they were remarkably effective in helping their children fulfill the American promise to a greater degree than they themselves realized. Because the *Issei* rarely talked about how much time and effort they spent on their children's upbringing, their achievement has not been duly acknowledged or appreciated by many people.

# Part I

## A Struggle to Build a Foundation

For young people in the 21st century, the 1880's seem long ago. They might say that it is ancient history, but the *Issei* - the first generation of Japanese who migrated to the United States - remembered the latter years of the 19th century vividly, because it was time when many of them left Japan to go to Hawaii and later to the United States mainland to start a new life. This new life was filled with *kuro*, (hardship and suffering), but most of them were accustomed to *kuro* because life had always been hard. They accepted their difficult lives and seldom expressed anger or bitterness about their circumstances. Very rarely did any of their children, the *Nisei*, (second generation) hear their parents whine or complain about their hard lives. Instead, they heard advice about overcoming life's hardships, along with repeated warnings to avoid the severe and demanding life that their parents had endured.

The *Issei* were born in the *Meiji* Era (1867 – 1912), a period of Westernization in Japan. The government pursued a modernization program to protect itself from European and American imperialism, but it was the people who carried most of the burden. The government imposed heavy taxes on the farmers in order to finance the industrialization and militarization of the nation. These instituted economic policies caused severe depression. As a result, the Japanese people, especially the farmers, constantly struggled and desperately looked for some kind of relief.

One young farmer who recalled his earlier days in Japan said, "I hated working in the rice paddies, always bent over, and many times I would be covered with leeches. I looked forward to going to school even though I had to study very hard. We rarely had time for play and the happiest time I had was at school, going to and coming back from school with my friends or my sisters and brothers." He also recalled, "I hardly remember eating any delicious, special food. But we didn't complain because all of our friends and neighbors lived the same way."

In desperate financial straits, many men left their families and went to nearby towns or cities to find work as migrant laborers. In the depth of this misery, the Japanese people heard about farmers who had been recruited to Hawaii to work as laborers earning fantastic amounts of money. They heard that they could earn one dollar (2 *yen*) a day for work which would enable them to save almost as much as a high level public official in Japan would make in a year. Spurred on by previously unheard-of rewards, many men, especially farmers, caught the fever to migrate. Accustomed to a harsh environment, they were confident that they could prevail over any kind of hardship. They planned to put in a few years of hard work in the promised land and then return home with money. Many young farmers repeated the stories that they had heard from other farmers which spurred them to make plans to go to America. "I can't believe that one could make so much money. I can't wait till I make the money and return home covered in glory (*nishiki o kazaru*) and pay off the family debt so my parents could hold up their head and be so proud of me!"

Furthermore, many men wanted to avoid conscription

into the Japanese Army. The government was becoming more and more involved in armed conflicts in China and later with Russia. "How would we get along, if my sons are drafted?" was the common cry of the poverty-stricken parents. Thousands signed up to go to America. For tiny Japan, it was a large number, but it paled in comparison to the mass of European immigrants who were dreaming the same dream.

## Early Racism

The *Issei* came to America with eagerness and excitement. At first, most of the *Issei* who had crossed over to Hawaii and America were single men, bent on making money quickly and returning home to solve the family's severe financial problems. However, their initial enthusiasm diminished as the days and years wore on. The reality of working in the United States was more forbidding than the young immigrants had imagined; the work was more physically strenuous than they were used to and they could not earn money as quickly as they had anticipated. Discouraged, many young men got caught up in the "sins" of gambling, excessive drinking and smoking, and cavorting with prostitutes. The few Japanese women who came to America during this time were young girls from desperate families who had sold their daughters to pimps. Sometimes they had been abducted or seduced by slick, greedy men with lies and false promises. One very young *Nisei* living in a boarding house remembered hearing some single *Issei* boarders talking in a loud whisper followed by muffled laughter. Not being able to hold his tongue, the youngster asked them, "Are you talking about *jyoro* (prostitutes)?" The workers were surprised, "How old are you? How come you know such a word like *jyoro*?" The young *Nisei* without a pause answered, "I'm six years old and everybody around here knows that word." Many Americans, particularly politicians and members of the labor and farm unions, soon used these signs of debauchery among the young immigrants to ignite an anti-Japanese movement, just as they had done against Chinese workers. The *Issei* had simply come at the wrong time. America was in the midst of an anti-Asian movement and discriminated against all people of color. Discouragingly, the racist movement was led by prominent politicians, including the governor of California, with support from almost every organization crucial to the welfare of the immigrants, such as the labor and farmers unions.

The Japanese government was well aware of this situation and made policies to try somehow to distinguish the Japanese immigrants from the Chinese. They tried to screen immigration applicants who were of inferior character to help maintain "Japan's honor." One of their early policies to improve the image of the Japanese immigrants and to promote a more stable *Issei* community in America was to encourage women to emigrate and start families in the new land, thus hoping to stem the immigrant workers' involvement with prostitution, gambling, and drunkenness. This new policy became an important factor when the Japanese workers found it almost impossible to earn their fortunes and return to Japan after a few years of work. Even though the work wage was higher than in Japan, the workers also had to pay for the passage to America, as well as their daily food and rent. Furthermore, much of the farm work was seasonal, so unless the farm workers followed the crop as itinerant farmers, they were not able to save enough money to return to Japan with a fortune as quickly as they had anticipated. Many were disappointed, and only a few were able to attain their dream and return to their home in Japan. Most of the men decided that they would have to settle in the new land, and they, too, began to think of establishing families in America.

Most *Issei* men followed the familiar custom of a marriage arranged with the help of family and relatives. The marriage was officially orchestrated by a matchmaker who tried to match the young people according to their family and personal backgrounds, their health, and their preferences. By Japanese custom, the intended couple usually exchanged photographs, followed by a meeting of the couple. Many *Issei* men made the long trip back to Japan to meet with the prospective partner, but in many cases, it was not practical or economically feasible, so couples relied largely on the photographs. Thus, these marriages were called *shashin kekkon* (picture marriage) and the brides came to be known as picture brides. Unfortunately, some men sent pictures of themselves when they were much younger, or a worker who was not confident of his own appearance might send a picture of another, possibly more presentable man.

Thousands of young Japanese women came to America filled with a sense of excitement and anticipation, but also filled with sadness, loneliness, and a great deal of anxiety about what was to come. The trip was a tortuous experience, cramped, smelly, and unsanitary. Many of the women were seasick and hardly left their bunks. Additionally, the food was terrible. Afterwards, many *Issei* women said that they would never ever go anywhere by boat. Years later, when the *Nisei* children of one family invited their *Issei* parents to go on a cruise, their mother refused, saying, "I told you that I would never go on a sea voyage again, and I meant it." The children tried to tell her that pleasure cruising ships were quite different from the smaller vessel on which she had come to United States, but she was not able to alter her unshakeable aversion to sea travel. (Curiously, this *Issei* lady was not afraid to travel by airplane.) There were few fortunate women who were able to travel in the first class cabins and luxuriated in a much more relaxed and leisurely voyage. Upon arrival, the misery continued for most of the *Issei* women, as they went through the immigration process in detention centers such as Angel Island in San Francisco Bay. "The place was awful. It was like a prison," said one weary traveler, "and I really hated the physical examination. Even the rice they served was nothing like I ever tasted, but fortunately, we didn't have to stay too long."

In spite of the hardships of the journey, the spirits of the travelers did not stay dampened for long. When they set foot on the American mainland, the feelings of anticipation and excitement returned in a rush. The *Issei* remembered the first days vividly. Everything seemed so fresh and new, and so different from their native country. They couldn't believe the size and the beauty of the new land. Everything seemed so large - the land, the houses, and even the people. They would learn later how immense the country really was. The buildings especially, seemed huge compared to those in Japan. Not even in Tokyo, their national capital, had they seen so many tall buildings. The American houses were so colorful. The newcomers had never seen houses painted in such a wide array of colors. The *Issei* expected to see big people in America; they had always heard that Americans had big noses, and they did! Equally interesting were people with red and blond hair, rarities in Japan. Furthermore, the women were dressed in colorful clothing all the time. In Japan, the women only wore colorful clothing on special occasions, and men always wore very plain, conservative clothing. The *Issei*'s senses were truly overwhelmed by the new country. Said one newcomer, "I thought that America was so big and beautiful, but the country and its people also smelled different.[3] They talked so loudly too!" That reaction was probably due to the fact that the first Americans the *Issei* met were officials or public employees who spoke loudly to people who did not understand English, mistakenly believing that raising their voices would improve communication.

Although the picture brides were delighted to reach their destination, they were understandably worried about meeting their future husbands, and with good reason. Many were men they knew only through stories or photos. The deceit of those men who had sent their brides old or fraudulent photographs now became clear. Some women were heard to say, "When I landed in America, there were many men waiting for their brides. I couldn't find my man until much later when I saw a completely different person carrying a sign with his name on it. What a shock! I was ready to get back on the ship and go back to Japan." Others noticed that the people they met were much older than in the photographs. Still more complained that their prospective bridegrooms were ugly, lacked dignity, or did not appear as well-to-do as expected. Some women had been married in Japan before they came to America, but even they were surprised to find their husbands were so different in their new country. One *Issei* wife said in shock, "My husband was so *sunao* (straight) in Japan, but when I came to America, I found that he had become a heavy, heavy chain smoker and a heavy drinker." Yet only a few women were so disappointed and angry that they returned to Japan, or ran off with other men. Most joined their new husbands and hoped for a life that was better than what they had left behind.

In an effort to cultivate a positive image, Japanese government officials actively sought immigrants who were willing to be Americanized, those willing to speak English rather than Japanese, convert to Christianity, and generally acculturate to American life. This strategy of Anglo conformity was designed to discourage the kind of treatment accorded to the Chinese, who seemed to make little effort to fit into their American environment. So, initially, there were some Japanese settlers who eagerly tried to become like the Caucasians they had met. They adhered to the old Japanese proverb, "gō ni hairaba gō ni shitagau"—the Japanese version of "When in Rome, do as the Romans do." Unfortunately, when they tried to enroll their children in elementary schools to learn English in cities such as San Francisco, Sacramento, and Walnut Grove, they found that their children were not even allowed to go to the same schools as the white students. They were shunted to a segregated school along with the Chinese. The segregation policy in San Francisco was rescinded only after a strong protest from the Japanese government and the intervention of President Theodore Roosevelt in 1906.[4] Yet, in truth, the Japanese government simply did not understand the racist attitude of the Americans in the late 1800's and early 1900's. In spite of governmental efforts, most Americans did not look at people of color as equals or as acceptable citizens, and discrimination in all sectors of life continued almost unabated.

In any case, the majority of the *Issei* did not follow the strategy of Anglo conformity. To start with, most of them had no time to learn English; they were too busy working. They also wanted to continue their Japanese lifestyle as much as possible. It gave them a sense of security and peace. Like the Chinese immigrants, they formed their own ethnic communities, building Buddhist temples, forming Japanese language schools and other Japanese organizations, and continuing to inculcate their children with the values and morals traditional to Japanese culture.

By 1900, there were about 24,000 Japanese immigrants living mostly on the west coast; this number grew to about 30,000 immigrants by 1905. Strong anti-Japanese policies adopted by the labor unions succeeded in steering most of the *Issei* into agricultural work. Although Americans made laws to prevent the *Issei* from leasing or owning land, the Japanese managed to become strong competitors to American farmers. This success further enraged Americans and led them to take increasingly harsh actions. "We knew how much they hated us," said one immigrant, "but we just kept working harder and vowed never to lose to the white people." Decades later, when the war against Japan began, some American farmers were in the forefront of the movement to evict the *Issei* from their homes and farms in California. The *Issei* were angry, but kept remarkable control of their emotions of anger, fear, and frustration, and were determined to continue to do their best under the circumstances. Many *Issei* women dreamed, as did one who said "My husband and I plan to save one thousand dollars and return home in glory. It's a matter of a little bit more patience and perseverance (*mō sukoshi no shinbō da.*)"

The discriminatory acts and the prejudice of late 19th century and early 20th century in America did little to discourage the *Issei* from their goal of making money. Because they were industrious, uncomplaining, and willing to work hard for low wages, the *Issei* were popular with employers,

MATSUKA

but the unions and the employee groups hated them. American employers soon found that the Japanese immigrants were willing to do almost any kind of work almost anywhere. Many found work as laborers on the railroads, in the canneries, in logging, and in the mining, meatpacking, and salt industries. Many *Issei* had been farmers in Japan, but when they came to America, many of them had to work as laborers in unfamiliar jobs and in highly racist surroundings which added to the stress. One *Issei* man who worked in a cannery talked about the time he had to fight a much larger Caucasian worker, "I couldn't back down when he picked a fight with me. I didn't care whether I got beat up or not." It was often difficult to keep up with bigger, stronger American workers. Only determination made the *Issei* succeed. One immigrant remembers, "We worked frantically and desperately because we were determined not to lose to the *hakujin* (white person)."

Most of the early immigrants came from an agricultural background so they often found work on the farms. Farm laborers were much in demand, and the wages were higher than at jobs they might find in the cities. Even more important, they were not required to have unfamiliar technical skills and did not need to make any kind of initial investment. The *Issei* worked hard and became valued farm workers. Typically, many of the *Issei* were not satisfied being common laborers and learned to handle all aspects of agriculture from farming to wholesaling. They hoped to acquire their own farms, even though Americans continued to try to block the purchase or lease of land to Japanese immigrants through legislative actions. Some *Issei* succeeded in purchasing land considered undesirable by Americans.[5] Through intensive farming, they eventually succeeded in becoming serious competitors, especially in truck farming. "The *hakujin* thought of many ways to keep us down," said one industrious Japanese farmer, "but that spurred us to greater effort."

The efforts paid off for some farmers. A few farm laborers saved enough money to live in the city and buy income-producing property. Others moved from farm work and sought urban occupations. As more Japanese immigrants moved into the cities, the natives in the cities began to resent the upwardly mobile *Issei*. Many started out by working in restaurants and soon learned to cook simple food to become short order cooks. Eventually, some saved enough money to buy or establish small restaurants of their own and did very well by offering cheap and convenient services. A *Nisei* remembered the first time he was taken to an *Issei* restaurant. "It was such a treat to eat away from home. Someone from our apartment complex owned a restaurant and from time to time, he would treat the three of us - my sister, my brother and me - to a simple roast pork dinner. I will never forget how delicious that meal was! And I shall always remember how dignified our neighbor looked wearing a white cook's cap and dressed up in the white cook's outfit."

## *Nihonmachi* (Japantown) and Small Business

As the number of Japanese families increased, there was an explosive growth of *Issei* business establishments. Small stores and shops multiplied. Laundries and cleaners, hotels and boarding houses, grocery, fruit and fish stores, drug stores, clothing and tailor shops, barber and beauty shops, auto shops, service stations and hardware stores successfully fulfilled the basic needs of the immigrant families. Other needs were fulfilled by art and curio shops, or by stores

selling pets, jewelry, cameras, books or furniture. "To own my own business was my dream for a long time," remembered one immigrant merchant, a sentiment expressed by many *Issei* entrepreneurs. These businessmen also provided many new jobs to fellow *Issei*, some of whom later started their own business.[6]

One of the greatest comforts to the *Issei* women were the services provided by the *sambasan* (midwife). Many of the *sambasan*, who had been trained in Japan, found it difficult to obtain the license required to practice in the United States, but somehow many managed to secure the necessary license. *Issei* women appreciated a midwife who could speak to them in Japanese and provide a greater sense of security about the process of giving birth. Furthermore, if a problem developed during pregnancy, the midwife served as a liaison to a medical doctor. So *Issei* women felt most protected and comfortable while in the care of the midwife for a week's stay at the *san-in* (maternity hospital) and had Japanese meals served to them. For many of the *Issei* women, the week's stay was like a vacation. The midwives found it personally satisfying to deliver a new baby in a new land and to enrich the lives of the immigrant families. A newborn child, referred to as *kodakara* (child treasure), was considered to be a blessed gift of the highest value. One *Issei* midwife who talked about her experience said, "I was so grateful that I was able to deliver new babies in this new land. I must have delivered at least half of the newborn babies in this community."

Gardening was another important occupation for the *Issei*. It was ideal because it required very little capital to begin and the gardener was his own "boss." An increasing demand for gardeners which provided steady and stable work for the *Issei*. At the same time, *Issei* women found work as domestic workers, and were sought by upwardly mobile Americans. Often, an *Issei* couple would work for the same employer.

At first, communication between American employers and Japanese workers was difficult, but the *Issei soon* learned enough English to provide high quality work for relatively cheap wages. As such, they were in constant demand. For the many newly rich Americans, having a Japanese gardener and/or a Japanese domestic worker was a prized status symbol. There was another beneficial aspect to the Japanese gardener phenomenon. When supplies such as plant seedlings, fertilizers and other garden supplies were needed, Japanese gardeners sought out nurseries owned by their country-men, supporting new Japanese enterprises in the process. At the same time, a greater demand for flowers meant that wholesale flower growers - many of them Japanese - also prospered. Before long, *Issei* began to occupy an important niche in the gardening and floral industry.

Many *Issei* gardeners spoke fondly of their experiences saying, "It was hard and demanding work, but it was also so satisfying to keep the gardens clean and beautiful." The

TO THE FLOWER MARKET

flower growers also took pride in their work which helped many people to share the beauty that they had created. However, not all *Issei* were so fortunate; many of them continued to work as laborers and domestic servants.

As more and more *Issei* moved into different cities, the Japanese settlements grew and they came to be known as *Nihonmachi* (Japantowns). Some of the larger Japantowns were found in San Francisco, Seattle, San Jose, Stockton, Fresno, Sacramento, and the largest one in Los Angeles was known as Little Tokyo. As the Japantowns grew at a rapid pace, more Caucasians came into contact with the growing numbers of *Nikkei* (people of Japanese descent). Many American consumers recognized that they were being better served by the *Nikkei* farmers, flower wholesalers, and importers of Japanese goods, and developed feelings of respect and friendliness. However, American business people who were in direct competition with the *Nikkei* were most angry and many of them carried out bitter, acrimonious attacks on the *Nikkei* which had a great influence in the incarceration of the Japanese and the Japanese Americans during the Second World War.

## The Depression

As fate would have it, in 1929, just as many *Issei* began to feel that their hard work and struggles had paid off, the United States and most of the world plunged into a devastating depression. Whatever gains the *Issei* made seem to vanish. Wages in some places dipped to an almost unbelievable 10 cents an hour, if one was fortunate enough to find work. Many of the entrepreneurial *Issei* were hit hard and lost their businesses. Characteristically, once again, *Issei* fought desperately to make certain that their children would never be trapped in poverty. "I never even dreamed that I would have to repeat this kind of *kuro* again," said one exhausted *Issei*. "I wondered if I ever would ever stop struggling." For many, their hard work resulted in building a strong foundation for their children. Even so, few imagined that they would have to face another devastating blow, one that was even greater than what they had already experienced.

## Onset of War

On December 7, 1941 most of the *Issei* and *Nisei* were likely enjoying a quiet Sunday morning, but the bombing at Pearl Harbor changed that forever. The Japanese immigrants in America and their American born children were particularly stunned. One *Nisei* remembered that on the Monday after the attack, his entire school was herded into the auditorium to listen to the speech by then-President Franklin Roosevelt. "Not many students and teachers spoke about the attack to me, but there was much tension and awkwardness in the air and I was very, very uncomfortable and nervous. Unlike some others, one of my Caucasian teammates never changed his attitude toward me and I really appreciated his friendship. The day before I left school, my English teacher stepped out as I was walking by and said to me 'I'm so sorry that war has broken out, but as far as I'm concerned, war is between countries and my personal feelings toward you as a student haven't changed. I wish you well in this kind of troubled time but do take care of yourself.' Her words meant so much to me."

Many other Japanese Americans, particularly those born in Japan, found that the animosity Americans had displayed to them in the past was significantly reinforced by the surprise attack on Pearl Harbor. Soon, many hostile and racist signs were visible all over American cities. Many Americans feared that the *Issei* were spies and that all

Japanese immigrants would actively help the Japanese war effort. These alarmists demanded that the United States government take some strong preventive measures. In the midst of such antagonism, there was much confusion, fear, and doubt in Japanese communities, especially among *Issei*. Their greatest fear was that they might be separated from their children who were mostly American citizens. A few thought that they would all be killed; but others had faith in the American government and believed that U.S. officials would not take any action against them.

The leaders of many organizations in the Japanese community were fearful of being arrested because they had heard that some leaders in San Francisco and Los Angeles had already been detained. Most of the leaders were already packed and ready to go to jail at any time. Generally the *Issei* remained overtly calm, although they were seething with anger, especially when they found out that after a series of confusing orders from the government that they would be evacuated to a government "camp" without adequate time to liquidate their homes or to attend to their financial affairs. Those who owned their homes and businesses were particularly angry that they did not have time to take care of their economic interests in a fair or reasonable manner.

As a result of the government's rash actions, the evacuees lost millions of dollars; in fact, most of them were ruined economically. While merchants and landowners suffered the greatest losses, bargain seekers swooped down on middle or lower income *Issei* to buy their personal household goods for a fraction of the market price. One *Issei* said, "My entire household goods were bought for $125 and my brand new Chevrolet was bought for $400." However, the most devastated were the families whose fathers were arrested by the FBI and sent to an unknown place. These "most dangerous enemy aliens", made up of local Japanese community leaders, Buddhist and Christian ministers and Japanese language teachers, were the first to be separated from their families, and incarcerated in a Department of Justice camp such as Roseburg, New Mexico. The families were not informed of their whereabouts, leaving the wives to take care of all the children, finances, and businesses, and later on to prepare to go to different concentration camps. Typical of many stories was that of a Buddhist minister's wife, whose husband was one of the first to be taken by the FBI. "All I could do at that time was to think of what I had to do," she remembers. "My first concern was, of course, for the four children I had who were all very young. How was I supposed to look after them in this critical time and see to it that they might lead a normal life? Second, I had to think of how I could help to close down the Temple without my husband and to consider the security of our Temple for the duration as best we could. And how was I going to take care of our personal belongings, and get ready to be taken into the government's custody? All I knew for certain at that time was that it would be a great challenge to me and I fervently hoped that I had sufficient spiritual strength to get through this critical time." One detainee who had been separated from his family recalled that he felt even more isolated and detached from his family after the second year because he could not imagine what his two youngest children who were born shortly before the imprisonment looked like. Constant and detailed news from his wife about the children did not clear away his sense of depression. "I never felt such loneliness in my heart."

As the United States government moved relentlessly and mercilessly forward with its plans to incarcerate the *Issei* and the *Nisei*, most of the *Issei* said, "Because I'm a Japanese citizen I can understand my incarceration, but to treat the *Nisei* as an enemy alien is unfair and inconceivable.

They should at least give the *Nisei* a choice of whether they want to stay with the family or not." A few families escaped internment because they had moved away from the West Coast prior to the evacuation order. Although they spent the war years in relative isolation and loneliness, most of them contributed much to the war effort. Regardless of how much suffering the order to evacuate caused, more than 100,000 Japanese and their American-born children, who were U.S. citizens, were incarcerated into ten federal concentration camps, euphemistically called "Relocation Centers" in one of the greatest miscarriages of justice in the history of the United States.

## Life in the Camps

Camp life was, at first, shocking; no one could have ever imagined that they would be confined to such stark and bare quarters. Most camps were in very remote areas, located far inland from the coast, often near deserts or swamplands. They were designed to be self-sustaining communities, so outside the barbed wire fences there was often land for farming vegetables. Hastily constructed barracks were laid out row upon row, built of boards covered with tarpaper. Inside the barracks were five single-room apartments, divided by partitions that often did not even reach the ceiling. Each apartment was furnished only with cots and blankets and a coal or wood-burning stove. In separate buildings, there were communal bathrooms with urinals, toilets, and a shower room, and a central mess hall for each of the housing blocks.

In spite of the bleak circumstances, the internees - in their most stoic fashion - soon set about making their surroundings more bearable. Homemade furniture began to appear, made by the men, and gardens, including Japanese style gardens, began to sprout near the barracks. The changes made the barracks seem almost like home, and many *Issei* simply said, *"sumeba miyako"* (If you live in a place long enough, it will become capital-like.)

After the initial settling down period, the camp lapsed into a fairly routine life. Most adults worked at the jobs that were necessary to keep the camp running as smoothly as possible. Most importantly, the young people started or resumed their school work. In spite of their crude and uncomfortable classrooms, the young people continued doing serious academic work, but also having some fun.

True to their upbringing, the *Nisei* did not forget studying. They were required to go to school, however poorly equipped and understaffed they were. Many of the Caucasian teachers who came into the concentration camps were dedicated, inspired, and motivated by the ever hardworking *Nisei* students. They were determined that when their confined students left the camps, they would be able to resume their studies and keep up with other students in regular schools.

One of the big and popular school events was the school dance. Even though the dances were held in the severe barracks setting, a little crepe paper decoration and eager young high school students made the dances lively and exciting. Not even the recorded music and the very modest refreshment diminished the eager, emotion filled young dancers. In fact, sports and dance proved to be the two most appealing and fun outlets for the *Nisei*. Baseball and softball championship games attracted a large crowd of fans, including a large contingent of *Issei*.

As for the *Issei*, many of them took advantage of the spare time they had by going to adult education classes to learn painting, writing poetry, or calligraphy, while others learned or continued to play *go*, a Japanese game played with stones, *shogi* (Japanese chess), or *hanafuda* (Japanese card game). *Mah Jongg* was another popular game that gave much pleasure to the participants. However, making the best of things did not mean acceptance. Many internees said, "How stupid that our government wastes so much money uprooting us and keeping us in camp and so many of us are just wasting time. Instead, they could have let us stay home where we really could have helped in the war effort."

The *Issei*'s attitude toward life reflected lessons learned from nature which helped them to survive the desultory camp life. They learned how to be flexible from watching the river flow over and around the different obstacles in its path. They also learned to be strong like the water and they often referred to the rain drops which can bore a hole in stone, or smooth the rough edges of stones. For example, to make the dingy and shoddy barracks more bearable, they managed to make Japanese gardens and build simple furniture from scrap wood. The people in Tule Lake and Topaz made lovely articles from sea shells, and the internees in Rohwer and Jerome made beautiful artifacts from Cypress trees. Many *Issei* artists looked at the dreary barracks that the government built along with the harsh, natural environment and managed to find bleak beauty within the camps.

Coming from a culture that put such faith in the power of hard work, many *Issei* parents worried that the uncharacteristically desultory life in the camps would have an insidious effect on the lives of their children and on the family in general. The parents worried that continued life in camp, in a state of limbo, would rob their children of initiative and a sense of purpose in life. Would life in the camps seriously erode the discipline needed to do well in life and would the family structure deteriorate? Much of the worry stemmed from the fact that the family hardly had any time together. In the communal dining halls, children often ate with their friends, and like teenagers everywhere, they were focused on fun. The boys were interested in sports and thinking about girls, and the girls were caught up in what was the most "cool" to wear to attract the boys. Generally, *Nisei* teenagers emulated the teenagers on the "other side of the fence" as creatively and as best they could within the severe economic limitations placed on them in the camps.

So, while camp life did not deprive young *Nisei* of the opportunity to continue their studies and socialize with their contemporaries, it did mean that they had little private time with their families. The tradition of talking together and learning from their elders was shattered by circumstance, and parents saw their relationship with their children slowly eroding. Many parents complained that, "If this kind of life continues, we will all decay as human beings (*ningen ga kusareru*)." The young *Nisei* adults, knowing that the internment would not last forever, also secretly worried about their life "after camp."

In the case of the draft age *Nisei* men, their options for the future were sharply limited when the military authority required them to fill out a "Loyalty Questionnaire." The answers to the loyalty questionnaire determined whether the young internee would be eligible for the military draft or not. It also could determine whether the young internee could be permitted to go to work or resettle in unrestricted areas of the United States, outside of California, Oregon, and Washington. The loyalty questions in the questionnaire caused an outburst of anger and explosive turmoil among the internees. "The government must either think that we are all fools," they said. "First, when the war started, they said that we were enemy aliens and hauled us into these damn camps. Now they decide that we are suddenly eligible for the draft because every loyal American citizen should be given the opportunity to serve the country." Outraged at the hypocritical nature of the questionnaires, the internees rightfully complained that other citizens were not required to answer loyalty questions when they were drafted. Many *Issei* parents were incensed with the latest government action and complained that "We have always taught our children that their country is America and that they owed loyalty to this country. The way they have treated our children is so senseless. Is loyalty a one way street?"

It was not surprising that there were a few draft-age men who expressed their anger by answering "no" to the loyalty questions. Among those who answered "no" were people who wanted to "fight back" and register their protest of the government's action. They wanted to tell the government that they would be willing to fight for our country as soon as their parents were released from the internment centers, but the questionnaire did not allow a qualified answer so many simply did not answer the questions or answered "no." Some others signed "no" because they wanted to keep the family together, especially those who had ailing or more aged parents. There were others who organized a protest movement against the unfair questionnaires, and the government in general. Others protested by openly resisting the draft and angrily protested the violation of their Constitutional rights.

Despite the shock, anger, and consternation the loyalty questionnaire caused, an overwhelming number of *Nisei/Kibei*[7] did declare their loyalty to the United States and subsequently volunteered or were drafted and served in the Army. Many of them were part of the 442nd Regimental Combat Team, one of the most outstanding and highly decorated units in the history of the United States, ultimately gaining deep respect from a grateful nation which had earlier treated them with suspicion, contempt, and injustice.

In the internment centers, those internees who refused to sign the loyalty questionnaire or who did not give any answer were classified as disloyal and were transferred, along with their parents, to the Tule Lake Internment Center which was redesignated as a special internment camp for the disloyal elements. Many who resisted the draft openly were sent to federal penitentiaries. There, until the war's end, many lived in conditions that were worse than their original camps. Simultaneously, many classified as disloyal were deported to Japan. Those who preferred to stay in America were permitted to do so. After all, America was their home.

## Starting Over

A sense of shock, confusion, fear, and doubt had enveloped the *Issei* and their children, the *Nisei*, when the war broke out between the United States and Japan. A similar sense of shock, confusion, fear, and doubt besieged them when the war ended and the government released and sometimes forced them from the internment camps.

The *Issei* recalled the first time they had to start from scratch in America. They had worried initially about how they would fit into the new world. They had known little of the lifestyle and culture of America. Most did not speak English or understood very little of America. Now, they knew a little more than when they first came to America, at least about the intense hatred that some Americans felt for the 'yellow skinned foreigners'. However, the recently released internees were again ready to do almost any kind of work, almost anywhere. They hoped this willingness would make them financially stable in a short time. Many were optimistic, energetic, and anxious to get to work as quickly as possible.

Unfortunately, the *Issei* who faced the prospect of starting all over again (*yarinaoshi*) from scratch after years of internment, were no longer the same men. While most of them had the same spirit as the first time they came to America and said, "I came to America with only my body (*hadaka ikkan*) and a strong will. I did what I needed to do, and I can do it again!" But they had aged and wistfully said, "I no longer have the energy and the strength that I had before." Their spouses and their children were aware that the person on whom they had relied for so long was no longer as dependable. There were some *Issei* spouses who did not have anyone to depend on because their partner had died in camp. Many *Issei* were sick or infirm by the time the government released them from internment. Some even hoped that they could stay in camp a little longer. But there was no option to do that. Thus, the more aged and ailing *Issei* faced the future with great doubt, fear, and pessimism, especially, the enormous task of finding a place to stay.

Establishing a new residence was a paramount problem for most internees. Very few had a home to which they could return. Those who did opened their hearts and their homes to those who were most desperately in need of a place to stay. However, the generous acts by these few compassionate homeowners could not help the vast numbers of returnees who were, essentially, without homes and without much money. The Japanese churches and temples did whatever they could, because they, too, were in dire economic straits. The best they could do was to offer a few families a place to stay on their premises. Equally important, though, they helped the returnees to find jobs or housing,

Many of the returnees received unexpected help from Caucasians. Most of the *Issei* were reluctant to return to their homes, particularly in the West Coast where they had been scorned and hated by hostile Caucasians. After being released from the internment centers, the *Issei* worried whether they would be subjected to the same kind of treatment. Many of them had heard rumors and reports about vandalism and abuses directed toward the first group of *Issei* who had returned to their homes, and, in truth, there were many merchants, restaurants, barber shops, and other business establishments who refused to deal with the 'Japs.' However, some *Issei* remember kind and brave Christian ministers who helped the struggling returnees by welcoming them into their churches and helping them to find places to stay and look for jobs. Sometimes they did so in spite of disapproving congregation members who criticized the ministers for helping the "former enemies." "We will never, never forget the kindness of these brave people," said one grateful *Issei*. A similar sense of gratitude was expressed by virtually all of the *Issei* families who received help from unexpected sources.

Some *Issei* found unexpected help from the unions which had generally been heavily anti-Japanese and anti-Asian before the war. There were many low paying jobs that Caucasian workers rejected in the post-war boom, and *Issei* snapped them up gratefully. They reasoned that even with relatively low paying jobs, they could save enough money and move up to better situations. "I was so grateful to find a job at a warehouse. Even though it was very hard work, I managed to earn some money for my family," remembers one appreciative *Issei*.

Others found jobs working as domestic helpers for wealthy families. Many *Issei* couples were hired by families that needed help inside the house as well as someone to keep up their gardens. Such couples endured these low paying jobs long enough to save enough money to rent or buy their own homes and then work independently as gardeners or domestic helpers. The *Issei* never forgot the people who helped them through the toughest years of starting over. In many cases, the *Issei* showed their appreciation by staying with the low paying jobs even though better opportunities were beginning to open up for the *Issei*. In later years, the Japanese community would hold an appreciation day for the people who helped them, a practice continued by the *Nisei*.

The *Issei* expanded on the help they received by regenerating their spirit and their diminishing energy to move up to higher economic and social levels. Families once again relied on their abilities to unite and work together. In cases where their husbands were ill or deceased, the *Issei* women carried the burden. Many *Issei* women worked in places they thought they would never work, such as in canneries. One of them recalled proudly, "I thought I would never work alongside white people, but I did, and I learned much about them as well as much about myself."

The *Nisei* and the *Kibei* were, perhaps, the most dependable contributors to the family effort. Many of them found work as domestic help, often called "school boys" or "school girls", to help alleviate the living expenses for their families or to help pay for college tuition. Also, because of their ability to function in English, they were able in many cases to help their parents expand family businesses. Others found employment which paid them much more than what their parents were able to earn, and their combined income allowed the family to build their economic foundation at a much greater pace.

Because the *Issei* parents had stressed the necessity and the importance of education to their children, many of them had gone to college or to specialized schools. Many *Nisei/Kibei*, therefore, were able to find relatively skilled positions in established firms or in civil service jobs. A great number of them went into teaching, and many went into engineering, accounting, dentistry, and medical fields. The *Issei* parents were deeply satisfied and extremely proud of their children's achievements, expressed simply, "All of our children really did well." (*Uchi no ko minna ga yoku yatte kureta*).

Although many *Nisei* and *Kibei* children enjoyed great success, there were many who sacrificed their personal careers in order to help their family. Many of the children hoped to continue their education beyond the secondary level, as they were taught and urged to do so by their parents, but in some cases, the immediate need to start over again required the children to stay at home and help their parents as best they could. Instead of going to college or a specialized school, many helped their parents reestablish their businesses or found employment as quickly as possible to help support the family. Most of those who had already finished college went to work as soon as possible instead of going on to graduate studies. Most children did not consider the steps they took to help the family as sacrifices, although their actions might have stopped or delayed their own careers. When the family situation was more firmly established, they resumed their studies in college or graduate school. Even more heartening was the fact that many *Nisei* women also extended their education beyond high school.

The *Issei* parents were deeply satisfied that their children were making their most cherished dream come true. Throughout the long struggle in America, the *Issei* did well economically, but were even more proud of the fact that they had kept their families intact and close. The *Issei* had surpassed the wildest expectations they held when they first landed in America.

# Part II
## *Issei's* View on Life and Parenthood

In trying to do the utmost to help their children attain their goals, *Issei* relied on the traditional method of rearing and educating children, the way they themselves were brought up.

The *Issei's* view on rearing their children was called *shitsuke*, a term made up of two words, *mi* (身) meaning self or one's being, and *utsukushii* (美) which means beautiful. Together, the two characters form the compound word *shitsuke* (躾) meaning child rearing. To the *Issei*, just rearing a child until adulthood was not enough. The *Issei* believed that an adult must be a fully self-supporting, beautiful person who is physically, mentally, and spiritually able to cope with the realities of life.

### Realities of Life

The *Issei* parents started with the belief that life was impermanent and unpredictable. "Nobody knows when he/she will die," and, therefore, a person should have a purpose (*mokuteki*) in life or a dream (*yume*) to sustain him/her through life. The purpose in life for the *Issei* was to do the best they could for the sake of their children (*kodomo no tame ni*). This phrase was repeated over and over again.

38

They said, "Our children are our treasure (*kodakara*). We must make sure that they grow up properly."

Of course, the parents did not often speak overtly about death but they made certain that their children understood that life was not only impermanent but also not always sanguine, optimistic or predictable. "*Jinsei* (life) is difficult to understand. That's why," the *Issei* parent would add, "you must take good care of your time and *mono* (things) and be grateful for the help you receive from others. They are too valuable to waste (*mottainai*)."

In the parents' strategy, step number one was to develop a healthy body. "*Kenkō daiichi* (Health comes first). Even if you're smart, you won't be able to do much, if your body is weak or sickly." Second, another important component to being a fully mature person, was to be mentally tough (*tsuyoi ishi*). "Once you decide what you want to do, you must not worry or fret too much (*kuyo-kuyo sezu ni*) and move forward." Then the child was further exhorted, "You must give your utmost effort (*doryoku*), persevere (*gaman, shinbō*) against all difficulties and do all things properly (*kichinto, tadashiku*)." Not only were the children constantly encouraged to endure and to put up with difficulties (*gaman*), but, above all, they were not to give up or lose (*makeruna*). "*Nani goto nimo makeruna!*" (Do not lose in anything!) These words of encouragement were spoken when it came to studying, and many *Nisei* heard their parents say, "*ketō/hakujin ni makeruna*" or "don't lose to the white folks." Although mental and spiritual toughness were stressed, the children were also expected scrupulously to "watch their manners." This was an important part of doing things properly (*kichinto tadashiku suru*). The parents also reinforced their teaching about enduring and persisting by working extraordinarily long hours to carry out their duties without complaint. They served as great models of the dictum, "Do as I do!"

Most of the *Issei* parents were not highly educated, although they may have been the best educated among all the immigrants who came to America to find a new life in the early 20<sup>th</sup> century. Most of the *Issei* agreed that the best way for their children to succeed in the United States was to obtain a good education. *"Kyōiku ga ichiban daiji da"* (Education is the most important).

The third step for the child was to develop spiritual strength (*seishin ryoku*). To the *Issei* parent, this meant that a person must be able to withstand life's unexpected "blows." "No matter how hard you try, sometimes things will not turn out as you expect them to. Sometimes there is nothing you can do to change that situation (*shikata ga nai*). Then you must have the wisdom and the strength to accept that." Further, the *Issei* parent counseled, "you must learn to accept reality (*akirameru*) and move on and do the best one can do (*dekiru dake no koto o suru*) under all circumstances. Remember how we have faced all kinds of unfair treatment and other difficulties almost all our lives, but we keep on trying to move on." Unfortunately, some *Nisei* remembered the term, *shikata ga nai* characterized only as negative and defeatist, but more than a few remembered how their parents had overcome numerous difficulties and challenges to survive in an unfriendly and hostile environment. Watching their parents, most *Nisei* learned to carve out productive and meaningful lives for themselves.

The *Issei*'s teachings were primarily intended to motivate their young children to do well in school, but the parents also expected them to apply themselves in other activities as well, such as sports. Many parents preferred the children to take up traditional Japanese sports, such as *kendō*, *jūdō*, or even *sumō* wrestling because they felt that these activities provided greater mental and spiritual training. However, they never insisted on having their way on everything because they believed that individuals do things well when they do things that are interesting and fun as well. Thus, when they saw their children prefer to play baseball, basketball, or football, most parents did not stand in the way. When they saw that their children were truly enjoying themselves, they asked only that their children retain the proper attitude, i.e., playing the games properly and earnestly and observing the spirit of sportsmanship and cooperation. The parents insisted that the children give their very best effort to do well and not give up. However, no matter how enthusiastically the *Nisei* youngsters pursued sports, they were always strongly reminded that "playing is all right, but you must not neglect your study."

## *Minna No Okage De* (With the Help of Others)

*Issei* parents tried to teach their children to be independent and hard working, but they also taught that an individual could not achieve any kind of success without the help of others (*minna no okage de*). To the *Issei*, this injunction included all beings. "All the human beings cannot live by one's effort only. To begin with, we live by the benefits received from countless lives of others (*minna no inochi*)." From the time a child could first begin to talk, they were taught to say a simple word: *arigatō* (thank you) followed by a simple bow of the head. By the time the child was an adult, the bow became a little more formal and the bowing became deeper. *Arigatō* was followed by other simple expressions. At meal time, the child was taught to say *itadakimasu* meaning, "I am grateful for what I am about to eat." When they finished, children were taught to say *gochisōsama* which meant, "thank you for the delicious meal that I just finished eating." As the child learned to understand more, the parents explained that *itadakimasu* and *gochisōsama* are actually words of gratitude we say to the animal, sea, and plant lives which were sacrificed for our meals and also to all the people who made it possible for us to eat our meal. That's why food is too valuable to waste (*mottainai*), so you must eat all of the food without complaint." Sometimes though, enforcing these concepts went to extremes. I remember a friend of mine telling me that she was struck by her father because she had spilled some rice when she was washing it.

The sense of *mottainai* was further reinforced when applied to clothing and shoes. Children were reminded to wear shoes carefully because so much sacrifice and work went into making and buying them. How many *Nisei* said, "I put in a cardboard paper when there was a hole in my shoe?" Countless numbers of *Nisei* children saw their mothers carefully wash and iron clothing, sewing on patches to get the utmost use out of them. The meager wardrobe of many *Nisei* children was well-worn and well-patched, but always washed, ironed and neat. This strong sense of *mottainai* was not always verbally taught, but the children could easily learn it from watching their parents save almost all durable things and recycle them for use in other forms. The children learned not to waste, but to conscientiously conserve the limited, valuable, and irreplaceable resources. The young children learned to express a strong sense of gratitude (*kansha*) to all those who helped them to develop and grow.

As the children matured, they were further told that the help they received was a debt and the individual was duty bound to repay (*orei*) the debt in some way. "If people are kind enough to help you, you must always show your gratitude (*kansha*)." Usually the word *on* (debt, benefit) was used to describe the help you received. The word *giri* (social and moral obligation) was used by the adults to describe

42

debt in a more profound manner. *Orei*, at the simplest level was simply saying *arigato* (thanks) but it became more and more involved as the person matured. The youngest were taught that their first debt was to their parents and that they should show their love for them (*oya kōkō* or filial piety) by trying consciously to live up to the standards established by the parents to become a responsible and productive person. The concept of *oya kōkō* to the parents was usually taught at school. Of course, many parents consciously reminded their children that they expected to be "looked after" when they became too old to care for themselves. Wherever they learned the term filial piety, as the parents became less able to care for themselves, the children tried to provide compassionate care and support as best they could. The phrase filial piety is rarely verbalized by the young in America.

The *Issei* parents also taught "Because of the teacher's help and kindness, you should never forget *sensei no on* (debt to the teacher)." At another level, the *Nisei* children were taught that they owed a great debt to their country and thus owed loyalty (*chūsei*) to it. During the Second World War, even when the American government had grave concerns about the *Nisei*'s loyalty to the United States, even going as far as violating the constitution to put them into concentration camps, the *Nisei* themselves had little doubt about their sense of loyalty. Anyone who understood the way the *Nisei* were brought up would have known that the overwhelming majority of them would have been loyal to the United States. Most of them had been taught that America was their country even though that might have meant that they might be fighting the Japanese. Almost all of the *Nihongo Gakkō* (Japanese Language School) teachers and *Issei* community leaders taught the same thing in no uncertain terms. Loyalty to one's country was only one aspect of repaying one's debt for valuable help provided to the individuals. The Nisei were also taught to be loyal to their family, friends, and community.

The *Issei* parents also tried to teach the intricate responsibilities required of all individuals to exist in an interdependent world. The *Issei* simply explained that we were "all in the same boat" (*minna otagaisama*) and therefore, we all need to work together in harmony with other people and seriously consider doing things for *hito no tame, yo no tame*—to work for the good of the people and good of the world.

The *Nisei* children were taught to become "Givers" rather than "Takers" as they matured. For example, they were encouraged to develop a spirit of cooperation (*kyōryoku*) to help create a strong and unified community, the kind of community which had been instrumental in ensuring the *Issei*'s survival and well being. The *Issei* also taught that the best way to attain cooperation was to be thoughtful and considerate of others (*omoiyari*). The *Issei* incessantly talked about making matters smooth and pointed out to their children that the character of the word peace (*heiwa*) was made up of two words - smooth and harmony combined. Helping to attain peace through harmony and cooperation was what the *Issei* parents meant when they said that individuals must work for the good of the people and world (*hito no tame, yo no tame*).

The *Issei* also tried to teach the importance of becoming aware of the many valuable benefits nature provided. The most obvious blessings were the food and the resources which all people depend on for their survival and well being. The *Issei* themselves practiced frugality and conservation and avoided unnecessary luxury and extravagance in food, clothing, and in lifestyle. They constantly urged their children not to be wasteful, but to treasure what they have and not get caught up in extravagance (*zeitaku*).

Another important idea of *Issei* parents was the belief that nature had many lessons to teach and that it provided much beauty which should be appreciated by people. Many *Issei* enjoyed reading and learning from the Japanese proverbs and poems; *haiku* focusing on nature. Countless *Issei*, especially women, composed wise and poignant poems and essays. Probably the greatest lesson the *Issei* learned from their understanding of nature is that no individual can ever take major credit for his/her achievement when it takes so much help from nature and so many other people. It was foolish for any individual to be arrogant or extremely proud of one's achievement so the *Issei* taught their children to keep a proper perspective about individual efforts and to develop a sense of modesty (*kenson*) and retain a sense of gratitude for all the help one receives. "Don't become a *rappa* (bugle) and blow your own horn," was the colorful way the *Issei* tried to implant the sense of modesty.

*Issei* parents often quoted *kotowaza* (proverbs) to make their point.[8] They would quote the following proverb to teach about modesty, "The more it bears, the lower the head of the ear of rice" (*Minoru hodo atama no sagaru inaho kana*). They also talked about how famous and successful people were brought up. General Nogi, a famed general during the Russo-Japanese War, was always used as an example of someone who hated certain foods when he was young and whose mother gave him the same food over and over again until he learned to eat all food without complaining. In this way, he learned the concept of *mottainai*. Another famous person often cited as a good model was Ninomiya Kinjiro. He was a poor farmer's son who worked hard but used his time wisely and never neglected his study. One of the most often repeated stories explained how he was sent to get firewood from the mountain, but he would also be reading a book to further his learning on his way up and down from the mountain. Later he became famous by practicing conservation of goods and money, doing good deeds anonymously, and continually doing charitable deeds for the unfortunate.

The children's reaction to parental instruction and discipline was, of course, varied. Many quietly acquiesced to their parents' words. There were others who never openly spoke up against their parents. "Most of the time I just did what they wanted me to do whether I agreed with what they said. Even when I disagreed I never said much to them and just kept my feelings to myself." There were those who were quick to express their disagreement, and some were openly rebellious. "I couldn't argue with them because I didn't know enough Japanese well enough, so I just yelled at them." Either way, the children remembered the many different methods of their parents to discipline them. When they were younger, many parents rewarded the "good" behavior with material rewards and punished a "bad" behavior by depriving them of material reward.

More often the parents resorted to verbal "reward" by praising the children profusely telling them how *rikō*(smart) they are. "I'm so proud when my friends tell me how *rikō* you are." A compliment based on what other people said was always more effective than just saying, "We're so proud of you because you are so smart," (or because you do everything correctly). And if they misbehaved or did not follow instructions, the parents would tell them to be more *sunao* (obedient). The children were deeply affected by the verbal approval or disapproval of their the parents. The parents were quick to praise the children for good behavior even in front of non-family members. This was pleasing and encouraging, but the children did not like to be compared unfavorably to other children. Even more uncomfortable were the occasions when parents would try to discipline them by saying that the continuation of a "bad" behavior would result in other people laughing at them. How many times did the *Nisei* hear their parents say to them, "If you continue to do *bakana koto* (stupid /foolish things) people will laugh at you?" Parents would also seek better behavior by telling their children that "If you continue to act foolishly the neighbors and friends will say that we are poor (bad) parents. Is that all right with you?" This was one of the most effective tactics used by the *Issei*. They stressed that no individual member of a family should bring shame to the family. Some of the children resented the sense of guilt implanted in them by this tactic. Conversely, a child who behaved well and brought praise to the family would have a greater sense of self esteem. One of the strongest message the *Nisei* absorbed was the counsel to bring pride and not to bring shame to the family.

Some very young *Nisei* were vividly affected by the horror stories told by their mother to reinforce their teachings. Some were told, "If you continue to do foolish things, I will have to send you to the circus or give you to the *kotori* (child takers)." "I didn't think that being sent to the circus was too bad, except that being away from the family was sad. But to be given to the *kotori* was horrifying. I just envisioned some big, ugly man putting me in a huge sack with all the kids inside going away from home to some unknown destination," recalled one *Nisei*, years later. Some parents resorted to punishing their wayward children physically, sometimes pinching their young children's arms and /or legs. On some rare occasions, father or mother, usually the father, would deliver a light slap to the face, but for a very rebellious youngster, a blow to the head was delivered with a *genkotsu* (a clenched fist). So a youngster reacted to and remembered the lessons of the parents according to how he/she was disciplined. Whether the parents were perceived as good parents or not, depended on many factors, such as, the abilities of the parents and children to communicate successfully verbally or physically.

Many *Nisei* with whom I have talked had mixed feelings about their parents. Some hated or strongly disliked their parents because they stressed the negative "stick" approach rather than a more gentle "carrot" method, although among them, there were those who acknowledged and even respected their parents' struggle and effort to "bring up their children properly." Many *Nisei* expressed "I wish that my parents would have shown more affection, especially by hugging me like the *hakujin* parents did." Many *Nisei* remembered their mothers as gentle and good because the mothers seemed to be the ones who were encouraging and more apt to appease them, and conversely, many felt that their fathers discouraged them by being too severe. Finally, many *Nisei*, as they grew older, and perhaps wiser, seemed to change their views about their parents, feel kinder toward them, and hold more respect for them. They would say, "It's amazing how strong and patient they were especially when they had to go through such difficult times in such a hostile environment."

## *Nihongo Gakko* (Japanese Language School)[9]

The language problem was a source of great frustration among *Issei* parents. Their children were equally frustrated since the language barrier meant constant misunderstandings and conflicts. Although the teachings of the *Issei* were simple, they were difficult to teach, especially when parents and children could not always communicate with each other as well as they wanted. Most *Issei* said that "We haven't got the time to study English, so if our children learn, at least, to speak Japanese that would help so much." Thus, the *Issei* in every community with significant numbers of Japanese Americans expended a great deal of effort, time, and money to build Japanese language schools to improve communication with their children.

The *Issei* also wanted their children to learn about Japan's culture. Most had been brought up in the *Meiji* Period (1867-1912), a fact of which they were extremely proud since this was a critical period in modern Japanese history when the Japanese started a concerted effort to catch up to the Western nations. Recently I visited an *Issei* lady who had just turned 101. She asked me if I had heard about General Nogi's meeting with General Stoessel of the Russian Army, a famous historic event from the Russo-Japanese War and then she recited the whole story. When I asked her if she remembered Emperor *Meiji's* Imperial Prescript on Education (*Kyoiku Chokugo*), she immediately recited the entire text. I was flabbergasted. Understandably, she said, "Of course, I wanted our children to share in the pride we had in our country. We were very proud to be a *Meiji no hito* (*Meiji* person)."[10]

Thus, the *Issei* began to build Japanese language schools in their communities. The first schools were established in Hawaii; six years later, in 1902, the first Japanese language school on the mainland opened in Seattle. By 1940, Japanese communities had established 282 schools in California, Colorado, and Utah and enlisted 295 teachers to teach 16,203 students. Buddhist Temples started the first Japanese schools but the Christian churches also sponsored schools. As time went by, the non-religious Japanese Language Association was formed and sponsored non-church based classes. Inspite of the fact that most of these Japanese language schools were built in the middle of the Depression, the *Issei* somehow managed to maintain hundreds of schools at a great cost to themselves.

A majority of *Nisei* attended the schools; unfortunately, the results were not what the parents had hoped for from their otherwise studious children. Reports that the children "did not study seriously" in *Nihongo Gakko* was probably because most classes were held after public school hours every day. Many *Nisei* said, "I'm only going to *Nihongo Gakko* because my parents want me to go, but going there every day after the regular school is too much for me." As hard working as *Nisei* students were, attendance at language school after regular school may have been too heavy an academic burden. Some Japanese schools were held on Saturdays, but that did not give most of the students enough time to learn the language effectively. Furthermore, to many *Nisei*, the school seemed foreign and old fashioned, partly because they were being acculturated in America by a stronger social force, including a notion that the Japanese language was not important. The *Nisei* may have concluded that only the truly important foreign languages, such as French, German, and even a dead language like Latin, would be taught in the American schools. Since the Japanese language was not taught, they may have concluded that the Japanese language was not relevant or important. One time I mentioned to a *Sansei* (third generation Japanese American) that her grandfather was highly educated and came from a distinguished family. His status was clear because in his passport he was described as a person of samurai lineage (*Shizoku*). Her response was, "Big deal! Look at him now, he's just a farmer and can't even speak English!" Ultimately, there may have been too many factors that deprived the students of any motivation to learn the Japanese language. Some parents were determined that their children should be fully integrated into American culture which meant that they did not encourage their children to speak Japanese. As a result, many *Nisei* did not learn enough Japanese to communicate fully with their parents.

However, merely by watching and listening to their parents every day, the *Nisei* absorbed many important lessons. For example, the *Nisei* learned how to express their appreciation to the *Shinbutsu* (the gods and the buddhas). The *Issei* who had converted to Christianity expressed their appreciation to God, and those who remained Buddhists expressed their gratitude to *Hotokesama* (Buddha). This meant putting into practice a belief that the individual not only had to discipline oneself to realize personal goals, but also to work for the common good, including the welfare of the environment, in order to exist in this highly interdependent world. Many of the *Issei*'s children, the *Nisei*, followed their parents' example.

## Enjoying Life

*Forgetting the hardship of pioneering,*
*Clapping and singing a tune in loud voices*
*and their cheeks so pink.*[11]

Although the lives of the *Issei* were filled with what seemed liked never-ending challenges, they believed that it was also important to live life joyfully. The *Issei* agreed fervently that "There are difficulties in life, but you must also learn to enjoy life." They believed that fun not only provided relief from their hard lives, but regenerated their energies. It was a way of showing that they could overcome hardship and hostility and continue with the lives they had planned for themselves.

The *Issei* knew how to pass their free time creatively and entertainingly. "It doesn't matter what you enjoy, but one must find something to enjoy." They engaged in leisure activities that ranged from the fine arts to the martial arts. Numerous *Issei* wrote poetry such as *Tanka*, a poem made up of 31 syllables; *Haiku*, a poem made up of 17 syllables; or *Senryu*, a satirical 17-syllable poem. Some painted in the traditional Japanese *Yamato* style or in the India Ink style of *Sumi-e*, or even in the more contemporary French style. More than a few *Issei* showed serious interest in photography. Many women practiced *Ikebana* or flower arranging while their husbands were dedicated to *Bonsai*, dwarfed or Miniature Tree in a Pot.

Some Japanese followed the elegant and complex practices of *Sadō* (Tea ceremony), or *Shodō* (Calligraphy). The musically inclined made music on traditional Japanese instruments such as the *koto, shamisen, biwa,* and *shakuhachi*. More athletic *Issei* and *Nisei* engaged in *Kendō* (Fencing), *Jūdō, Kyūdō* (Archery), or in *Sumō* (Japanese wrestling). Those interested in dancing engaged in Japanese Classical or Folk Dancing or even *Kenbu* (Sword Dancing). Others found great pleasure in chanting Shigin (chanting of Chinese style poems), *Utai* (chants from the Nōh plays), or in singing *Nagauta* (songs usually sung with *Shamisen*). The *Issei* who preferred to play games were absorbed in *Go* (board game played with stones) or *Shōgi* (Japanese chess). Another popular game was *Hanafuda* (Japanese Card Game) but equally popular, especially among men, was poker. *Mah Jongg*, was also widely and wildly played by the *Nisei* in the concentration camps. Often, the *Issei* who engaged in these pursuits formed organizations and clubs based on their favorite leisure activity.

Another organization which provided much joy was the *kenjinkai* (prefectural club), an organization comprised of immigrants from the same prefecture. The members considered each other extended family, supporting each other in time of trouble and celebrating together on special occasions. The club was indeed a home away from home. Many of the *Nisei* have continued the *kenjinkai* started by their parents and continue to share in good times and bad. In all of the special interest clubs and organizations, the members had very close personal relationships and they strengthened their bonds by observing special holidays throughout the year. Most of the family members and friends remember these events with a great deal of nostalgia and acknowledge that these experiences served to unify, strengthen, and deepen the family and community ties. Many *Nisei* still cherish the occasions when they saw their parents cast aside their usual serious demeanor and show their most relaxed and joyful selves.

## Community Spirit and Cooperation
### *Oshōgatsu*

One of the most special of occasions came at the beginning of the year: the *Oshōgatsu,* New Year's celebration. Preparation for it began days before. Homes were thoroughly cleaned to welcome the New Year and get rid of the 'old year's dust'. Efforts were made to pay off as many debts as possible. Elaborate meals were prepared days ahead of time, sandwiched between busy working schedules. One of the most lighthearted occasions was the making of the rice cake called *mochi.* Usually a few families got together for the day-long pounding (*mochitsuki*) of special steamed, sweet rice into a hot sticky paste. Everyone, including young people, took turns pounding the rice. The procedure required a great deal of coordination as two men pounded the sticky sweet rice and the third person slapped water into the *mochi* rice to prevent the *mochi* from sticking to the stone bowl before the wooden pounding mallet came down. When the rice was ready, the women and the children molded the rice into different sized balls and patties. Usually, larger sized *mochi* were used for display or offerings. Two *mochi* cakes, stacked together and decorated with *kombu,* dried sea weed or kelp, that symbolized happiness, *ika,* a giant dried squid or a cuttlefish, for wisdom, and a *mikan,* tangerine for the generations of people in the family. This was displayed or offered as a symbol of gratitude and good luck. The *Mochitsuki* tradition was laborious, but it was also fun and it created much goodwill among the participants.

On New Year's Day, everyone ate the traditional *Oshōgatsu* breakfast called *ozōni* (*mochi* soup), which was supposed to bring the luck and strength needed to sustain one through the year. The highlight of New Year's Day was the elaborate and delicious evening meal called

*Oshogatsu gochiso* or *Osechi Ryōri* (Festive New Year's Food), miraculously prepared by the mother and her older children in spite of an unbelievably busy year-end schedule. The traditional feast included *kuro mame* (black beans) which were supposed to bring good health; *tai,* carp symbolizing strength and determination; *renkon* (lotus plant) representing the "beauty growing out of mud" concept; *kazunoko* (herring eggs) for fertility; wrapped kombu (sea weed, kelp) signifying happiness, *sato imo* (*taro*) to drive away evil spirits; and different kinds of *sushi, sashimi,* and vegetables.

During New Year's Day, the head of the family would visit the homes of friends to exchange New Year's greetings where he was royally wined and dined. By the end of the day, when he returned home, he was extremely light headed and well lit up. An often-told story involved a guest, well known for heavy drinking, but not for his ability to hold his liquor, who was mistakenly served vinegar instead of *sake.*

Fortunately, he did not notice the difference and went happily home after thanking the hostess profusely for the warm
treatment he had received.

Of course, the women of the home stayed home to greet
the guests who came to exchange New Year's greetings, but
the mother also usually managed to spend some time with
her children. One of the games played by many *Issei* family was called *Karuta*, a game made up of many different
proverbs. As they were read, the participants tried to find
the correct card from many different cards spread all over
the floor. The person who collected the most cards won.
The best players usually memorized the proverbs so that
they could identify the proverb by the time the first syllable
was read. For children, it was also a time to receive New
Year's gifts (*otoshidama*). Gifts were exchanged by adults as
well. In most Japanese communities, the family merrymak-
ing continued for three days. Because various community
organizations as well as families would hold a New Year's
Party (*Shinnenkai*), the whole month of January became one
long New Year's celebration.

Many third and fourth generation Japanese also continue
to celebrate Thanksgiving and Christmas holidays, as well,
regardless of their religious or ethnic backgrounds. As an
American tradition, family members from far and near make
special efforts to assemble at their parents' homes, yet their
heritage gives a special flavor to the traditional holiday feast.
In Japanese homes, additions may include plain boiled rice
(*gohan*) as well as some fried bean curd sushi (*inari-zushi*)
and rolled sushi (*maki-zushi*).

There were two other widely celebrated year-end parties.
One was a Respect the Elders Party (*Keirōkai*) organized by
the younger *Issei* who wanted to show their appreciation
and gratitude to the older *Issei*. The second was the Forget
the Old Year Party (*Bōnenkai*). These parties became popular

after the internees were released from the concentration camps. In some communities, the *Keirokai* and the *Bonen-kai* were held simultaneously. In smaller communities, the Japanese custom of paying off all the debts and finishing all the unsettled business by the end of the year was often mixed with the New Year's party (*Oshōgatsu*) so that the people could forget the unfortunate and negative events of the past year and start the New Year with a happy frame of mind.

## *Obon* Festival

Another widely anticipated community event was the annual *Obon* festival which was held in various Buddhist communities in July or August. It was a Buddhist event but the entire community, Buddhist or otherwise, took part in the *Obon* dances, the festive portion of the *Obon* observance. In Stockton, for example, one of the most eager participants was a prominent Christian who was famous for his deliberately comic style of dancing that added special flair and spark to the dances. The traditional dress for the dancers was the colorful informal summer *kimono* called *yukata*. However, many young people wore the formal and more elegant long sleeved *kimono* called the *furisode* because they had almost no opportunity to wear them in America. Visitors from Japan often looked at these elegantly-dressed young dancers with amusement, not knowing the reason why the young dancers chose to wear the more exquisite outfit.

At first, the *Obon* was limited to a religious service and the *Obon* dance (*Obon Odori*) was the event that attracted the most public notice, but later, to raise money to maintain their temples, temple members expanded the event and began to sell food, handicrafts, *Bonsai* plants, and flowers.

They also planned cultural events, added games for children, and turned the festival into a two-day bazaar which attracted community-wide attention. To prepare for such a large scale event, temple members and their friends constructed various booths and prepared food days ahead of time.

The main event of the two day bazaars remained the *Obon Odori*, and the participants, both Buddhists and non-Buddhists, *Nikkei* and non-*Nikkei*, increased and turned the bazaars into major community events. *Nikkei* went to other bazaars during the *Obon* season to check out their food, program, and dancers, and inevitably, each Temple member felt that their own bazaar was the best.

## Weddings

*Issei* wedding celebrations also produced more good times and merriment. The wedding ceremony was generally held at a church or a temple. The guest list was usually very long because relatives and all the friends who had been helpful to the family were invited. There were simply no small weddings. The reception was often held at a local Chinese restaurant. The reception was divided into two parts. The first part was the formal part when the married couple, the wedding party and the relatives were introduced. Then representatives and friends from both families delivered appropriate words of greeting and felicitation. Solemnity and formality marked the first phase of the celebration (*isshiki*). Then the mood changed abruptly to an almost raucous atmosphere in the second part of the ceremony (*nishiki*). There was much drinking and shouts of goodwill and a time provided for guests to entertain the newlyweds and other guests. It was surprising that so many people would get up and sing or tell stories or deliver humorous advice to the newlyweds. The usually serious *Issei* would throw inhibition to the wind and let themselves go. The next day, when they went back to work, they exhibited their customary serious demeanors as though the good time they experienced the night before had never happened.

Even for the *Nisei* generation, the wedding ceremonies generally followed the same traditional pattern. During the first half, the newlyweds were introduced, followed by a tinkling of the glassware to urge the newlyweds to kiss each other. Then the families and relatives were introduced, followed by words of congratulations from the best friends of the newlyweds in English, of course. Throughout the dinner there was more tinkling of the glassware and urging for more kisses by the newlyweds, stoically watched by the *Issei*. In the informal second half, after some entertainment by the guests, most of the time was spent dancing by the newlyweds and the guests, again, impassively observed by the *Issei*.

## Japanese Movies

Other organizations in the *Nikkei* communities began to plan additional community activities. For instance, Japanese movies were shown by individual promoters who went from town to town with films imported from Japan. In the early days when the movies were 'silent,' these promoters became narrators and voiced all the actors' roles in the movie. Some were adept at speaking women's, men's, and children's roles, but many of them were not as talented. Some made no effort to distinguish male and female voices; one memorable narrator explained that he was going to read the dialogues in one voice and ended by saying in thick Japanese accent, "That's all right." What delighted the audience was the fact that he wore the outmoded top knot hairstyle (*chonmage*) of the traditional *samurai*.

Usually, two features would be shown, one modern picture and one samurai film with plenty of sword fights (*chambara*). The younger people loved the action filled *chambara* films, and *Nisei* learned the names of the popular *chambara* stars such as Bando Tsumasaburo, Okochi Denjiro, and Kataoka Chiezo, but they also looked forward to seeing such modern picture stars such as Kurishima Sumiko, Tanaka Kinuyo, Oka Jyoji, and Uehara Ken. Going to see these Japanese movies turned out to be a major community event as young and old friends came together, brought refreshments, discussed the movies seriously, and generally had an enjoyable time and looked forward to the next movie presentation.

However, these movie nights gradually disappeared as older *Issei* passed on and fewer young people went to see them. Whatever interest the *Nikkei* now have in the Japanese movies are for acclaimed films that are played in the regular theaters. More avid viewers can now depend on watching contemporary films on television, but they are limited to cities with sizable ethnic audiences. Occasionally some community centers, senior centers, and temples might have a video showing of the classic Japanese films which attract small, but enthusiastic *Nisei* audiences. To the rapidly decreasing *Nisei* people, the vanishing of the old community movie night remains a nostalgic and poignant memory.

## Fishing and Picnics

Another enjoyable activity for many *Issei* families was the fishing trip they took in the summer. In some families, the entire family went fishing, but the father was the busiest person, especially when there were very young children involved. He had to get everything ready so that the only

thing the children had to do was fish. The most hectic part was when the very young and inexperienced ones caught a fish. Then the father had to rush over to the child and give frantic instructions or finally bring in the fish himself. The worst part for the father was the clean up time after the fishing trip. The caught fish were put into a gunny sack which became muddy, wet, and smelly. Usually the children hated sharing a ride with the smelly catch, but even worse was cleaning the fish once they got home. After scaling the fish and cutting off all the unnecessary parts of the fish, many young children learned to hate eating fish. Others learned to love the taste of a very fresh fish and savored that flavor throughout their lives.

Although the time for having fun with the family did not happen as often as the children wanted, perhaps, because of the infrequency, they truly learned to appreciate the time with their family, and many remember those occasions

vividly and fondly.

Another special day of fun for most of the *Nikkei* families was the Japanese community picnic usually held in the summer. For the young people, it meant a full day of foot races, relays, *sumo/kendo* matches, and the opportunity to eat mountains of picnic food. The picnic came in a box or basket and was thus called *Obento*, but in fact, it rivaled the elaborate New Year's feast. For the older people, the occasion was a time to talk to old friends and make new acquaintances as they moved from family to family, drinking wine and tasting the different families' dishes. The climax of the picnic was a kind of a masquerade costume parade where the *Issei* competed with each other to wear the most outlandish and comic costumes. Young people rarely saw their parents so relaxed and carefree, and years later, many *Nisei* still treasure this rare image of their parents.

## *Kodomo no Tame Ni* (For the Sake of the Children)

The *Issei* parents' lifelong ambition to do the best for the sake of their children meant that they taught them that life was unpredictable and tough. They insisted that their *Nisei* children, in order to be fully mature and productive individuals, must learn to be physically, mentally, and spiritually tough by working hard and persevering inspite of obstacles that might stand in the way of achieving their goals. The *Issei* tried to teach their children to be flexible, tolerant, respectful, and appreciative of the sacred worth of all living things and maintain strong religious faith and a sense of cooperation, thereby nurturing their families and promoting community unity.

The best way, however, to determine how well the children learned their parents' teachings is to examine what they did when they matured into adults. The result of the *Issei* efforts was one of the most remarkable generations of people in American history, the *Nisei*. *Nisei* built on their parents achievements in the fields of small business, gardening, and agriculture and reached remarkable levels of success. They outstripped almost all other ethnic and cultural groups and rapidly expanded into the professional fields such as teaching, dentistry, optometry, engineering, and architecture. Additionally, compared to other ethnic groups, the *Nisei/Kibei* had the lowest rate of criminal behavior, delinquency, and mental illness. During the Second World War, the *Nisei/Kibei* left an unmatched record in the military. Their struggle to restore their civil and constitutional rights has been historic. The *Nisei/Kibei* have marched for world peace and have participated in anti-war demonstrations as well as taken part in movements to extend civil liberties to powerless and underprivileged people. *Nisei* have generally elevated their own social and economic status.

In a 1984 speech, President Ronald Reagan recognized America's rich and diverse heritage and praised the Asian Americans, including the Japanese Americans, for helping to preserve the American Dream by living up to the bedrock values of America. Many *Nisei*, however, did not accept the "model minority" image because they felt that they were still not treated as equals and that racism continued to prevent this remarkable group from achieving full equality. Many *Nisei* also felt the "model minority" image was misused against other ethnic minority people and created unnecessary misunderstanding directed against the *Nisei*. What *Issei* parents wanted for their children and taught them was not significantly different from what most other parents anywhere wanted and taught.

The difference in the result may have been in the fact that the *Nisei* children could really believe that their parents tried to do everything for the sake of their children. For the sake of the children (*kodomo no tame ni*) was a mantra among the *Issei*, and the *Nisei* could see that their parents meant what they were saying. They saw their parents work, work, work, scrimp and save, scrimp and save, hardly ever going on vacation or spending extra money on themselves. They could clearly see their parents trying to live up to the standards they were trying to teach their children. The *Issei*, by and large, were peerless role models.

# Part III
## Growth of the *Issei*

*Issei* parents were ideal teachers who conveyed the best of their cultural values to their children, but they were also dedicated learners. The long years in America taught them about the best of America; they assimilated these new American values into their lives.

In the early 20th century, when the *Issei* heard that America was a great land of opportunity, they emigrated in droves, and, for the most part, they were not disappointed. They found that in this rich country (*Beikoku*) on many levels, the fabulous stories were true. Despite the hostile and harsh treatments they received, they learned that they, like other immigrants, could earn a piece of the American Pie. Although the share might not be commensurate with their effort nor with the amount of abuse they received, they were convinced that, in spite of prejudice and discrimination in America, their children would have better opportunities to achieve their personal goals than they would in Japan. The *Issei* reasoned that if they could improve their status as immigrants to America—without citizenship and almost no knowledge of English—then their children, who would be educated citizens of the United States, would have an even brighter future in America. Many *Issei* agreed that "When our children become *ichininmae* (fully grown, self supporting person) they certainly will have a better life. They certainly have more advantages than we did. I could hardly wait for that to happen." They also knew that it was not going to be easy and told their children, "You must continue to work and study even harder, and you must never forget our spirit to never lose in anything."

One of the reasons for their optimism was the idea of equality, a feature of Amercan life that had attracted them to the country. Most of the *Issei* came from poor, rural communities where they were considered common people (*heimin*). As such, they saw very little possibility of being treated equally in the tightly drawn hierarchical society of which they were a part. The lines between the higher ranked people—made up of former warriors, nobles, and rich merchants and professionals—and the commoners were tightly drawn and observed. For example, the commoners had to speak in a more courteous and higher level language (*keigo*) to those above them, and the people of higher station spoke down to the commoners in less than polite words. The commoners, which included most of the *Issei* immigrants, for the most part, spoke regional dialects (*hogen*) instead of the standard Japanese (*hyojungo*). The class-conscious Japanese were especially disdainful of people of Okinawan, Korean or Eta backgrounds.[12] Oft repeated by the *Issei* was the following sentiment, "Sometimes I miss my family in Japan and our native village but it's so hard to live over there. Most of all, you have to be careful how you speak to a person. You have to be so aware of your position and the other person's position and speak accordingly. It's so *urusai* (bothersome)."

When the *Issei* came to the United States the rigid social hierarchy of Japan started to dissolve. From the beginning, the *Issei* noticed that Americans generally spoke in the same way to almost everyone. They were amazed to see workers express their feelings frankly to their bosses and even talk back to them. Of course, they noted that there was still a line between the authorities and the workers, but no one bowed and scraped as the Japanese workers had done in Japan. Thus, when they worked with their fellow *Issei*, even if they came from different social and economic levels, they learned to relate to each other more equally. This trend was reinforced because cooperation was essential if they were to overcome the hostile treatment they received. Thus, with a new sense of confidence and self-esteem, in this new country, the former commoners began to feel much less intimidated by others even the "new upper class" *Issei*.[13]

Another example of how the *Issei* loosened their traditional attitudes can be seen in their ideas about marriage. Traditionally, parents and relatives had a strong influence on their children's marriages. At first, in America, *Issei* parents hoped that their children would marry someone from a family who came from the same prefecture and shared the same religious views. "If it is possible, we would like *uchi no ko* (our child) to marry a *dokenjin* (a person from the same prefecture). We also would prefer someone who went to the same church/temple." Although they could not dictate all the conditions for the marriage of their children, the parents of the earliest *Nisei* children had enormous say in choosing their children's life partners.

According to Japanese tradition, matches were arranged by a family friend or a go-between (*baishakunin*), a person who knew the two families intimately. Thus, many of the daughters married someone who was thought to be the best person for her. Often she was introduced to the prospective partner for the first time at an arrangement (*miai*) made by the go-between. Although most young *Nisei* daughters had the chance to make the final decision, many of them simply complied with the parents' wishes, sometimes marrying a man from Japan or a *Kibei* or someone who was much older than she. And, in many cases, these marriages turned out to be as successful as the go-between had predicted.

As time went by, these arranged marriages became more and more rare. The parents found that their children did not necessarily want to marry children from a particular prefecture or someone who belonged to the same church or temple. The parents did not feel too upset if their children did not pick someone from the same prefecture, but they were generally disappointed if the potential partner did not go to the same temple or church. Reluctantly, they learned to be satisfied as long as the partner was a Japanese American and a nice person with a good education. Eventually, many *Nisei* refused to be limited to choosing someone of the same ethnic background and began to look for a more suitable partner regardless of their ethnicity. "We can accept my child not marrying a person from our prefecture or marrying someone from the same church/temple, but he/she must marry a Japanese," the *Issei* parents would demand adamantly.

Their children could be as determined as their parents and some insisted on marrying someone of their choice until the parents eventually gave in. Usually, the first outside marriage were to Caucasians a more acceptable alternative than other non-Japanese ethnic group to the *Issei* parents. Even though they had experienced ethnic discrimination, the *Issei* had their own prejudices. Caucasians were bad enough, but even worse was marrying a Chinese , a Filipino or another Asian. The most unacceptable, certainly, were Hispanics and African Americans, but all of these prejudices were overcome eventually because the *Issei* had always been able to accept changing conditions and realities. As always, their immense love for their children was paramount, and they did not want anything to stand in the way of their eventual happiness. Thus, previously shunned people became part of *Issei* families. The early reluctance quickly melted when the first grandchild arrived. "Babies are without fault or sin," said the *Issei* grandparents, "and so when I carry my grandchildren they are so innocent and adorable."

Today, over 60 percent of Japanese Americans marry non-Japanese Americans. Few remaining *Issei* that I have known have even learned to accept same sex marriages, simply saying, "Even if we don't like it, there's nothing we can do (*shikata ga nai desu ne*). Conditions of life certainly do change a lot (*Jinsei wa yoku kawaru mon desu ne.*)"

What is truly amazing about the *Issei*'s change of attitude about marriages for their children is that it generated a change in their prejudices toward 'undesirable people' within the span of a single generation. Prejudice has marred the history of the United States for hundreds of years and it is still a major social problem in our country today, so it is truly remarkable that the great number of *Issei* changed their views about racism in one short lifetime. Needless to say, however, there are still many Japanese and Japanese Americans harboring racial and ethnic prejudice. Although many *Issei* changed their views about mixed marriages, many people, including the *Nisei*, continue to think that the *Issei* were old fashioned and hopelessly out of step with the society.

Over the years, the *Issei* learned to accept the fact that their children had different wants and needs. They no longer insisted, for example, that the oldest son should continue the family business as tradition would have demanded. However, the *Issei* did demand that their children do well in school and that their sons go beyond high school and choose an occupation that would be good for the people and the world (*hito no tame, yo no tame*). For many years, they raised strong objections to allowing children to go into the fields of sports or entertainment. Many very talented *Nisei* athletes, who had not been allowed to pursue their athletic interests, were truly envious of the very few *Nisei* athletes who became college standouts or even professionals. So, when the *Nisei/Kibei* became parents, many of them encouraged their children and grandchildren - the *Sansei, Yonsei,* and *Gosei* (third, fourth, fifth generation *Nikkei*) - to pursue careers in sports, movies, dance, or music.

In general, the *Issei* expected their sons to go to technical schools or college. Although they were always struggling economically, most tried to make certain that at least the oldest son would be able to go to college. However, in many cases, they allowed other children, including the girls, to further their education if they were willing to work to pay some of the expenses. Thus, many of the children worked part-time, sometimes as domestic workers in return for room and board, and struggled to get as much education as possible. *Issei* parents helped where they could, even if it meant working even harder. They were willing to make such sacrifices because they were convinced that their children would do better socially and economically than they had.

The *Issei's* ultimate growth was in their acceptance of the reality that their children had fully matured to become productive and useful members of society, just as they had wanted them to be. They were able to "let go" of their children with deep respect and love.

# Part IV
## *Issei* Cultural Values [14]

*Issei* parents were eminently successful in helping to develop their children (*Nisei*) to become fully mature and productive citizens by instilling values which will be briefly summarized here.

### Acceptance of the World

Generally, Americans believe that they can solve any problem, that they have the ability to control even nature by eventually unlocking all of her secrets. They abhor paradoxes, irrationality, and anything that is not clear, well defined and capable of determination. However, the *Issei*'s view was sharply different. They felt that life was ever changing and therefore unpredictable. They simply accepted life as it was with all its contradictions, confusion, absurdities, and mystery, but that did not mean that they never planned for the future or worked hard to reach their goals. As noted earlier, the *Issei* faced and accepted three major changes brought on by forces beyond their control - racism, economic depression, and war. Their attitude was, "Hardship (*kuro*) is one of heavy load (*omoni*) one must carry in life," or "Life is one of continuous hardship." (*Kuro no renzoku da*). They accepted such interruptions as reality and focused on the immediate task before them.  They were also able to value and appreciate the moments that offered them relief, hope, and enjoyment.

## Borrowing and Innovation

The Japanese learned from their life's experience that they could improve their lives if they borrowed ideas from other people who had good ideas or better ideas.  For example, the Japanese had borrowed religious ideas from the Chinese and adopted Confucian, Taoist, and Buddhist teachings, and in a more modern period, willingly accepted Christianity. They also made large scale efforts to learn science, technology and the languages of the Western nations, especially English, in an effort to make their country prosperous and strong enough to resist the exploitation of Japan by foreign powers.

When the *Issei* immigrated to the United States, they quickly learned to borrow the best of America.  Many of them converted to Christianity and learned English.  Some of these *Issei* refused to have their children learn Japanese and urged their children to become proficient in English. "You don't need to learn Japanese because you're in America.  Learn English and do well in school!"

It was also no surprise that most of the *Issei* parents urged their children to learn the best from American education and make studying their first priority to escape poverty and build up their self esteem.  "Your job is to study and do well in school," the *Issei* parents would insist in no uncertain terms. They also struggled to enable their children to go beyond high school and attend colleges or technical schools.  Thus, many of the *Nisei* went on to study science, and technology and became engineers, doctors, ophthalmologists, optician, pharmacists,  teachers, and technicians.

As the Japanese borrowed from other people they also

modified and integrated what they borrowed into their own culture. They selected those elements that fit best into their life-style, and thus, maintained a distinctive Japanese "flavor." Shinto religion is thought to be indigenous to Japan, but actually, it is a combination of Buddhist, Confucian, and Taoist ideas. The Tea ceremony and flower arrangement, both borrowed from the Chinese, were modified in form and techniques so that they differ significantly from the Chinese way. Similarly, they made innovations and refinements in modern times in electronic products, automobiles, and railway systems. When baseball became popular in Japan, the Japanese added the practice of having the two competing teams face each other and bow because the Japanese tra ditionally always had competitors perform some kind of a ritual to show respect for each other.

When the *Issei* came to America, they continued this mode of innovation and integration. For example when their *Nisei* children began to take up American sports, the *Issei* added a strong emphasis on the spiritual aspect of the games and an insistence that their children exhibit sincere effort and discipline, courtesy at all times to other players and officials, and good sportsmanship

## Preserving the Best of the Past

There is a famous proverb that many Japanese follow: "To study the past to understand the new" (*onko chishin*). The Japanese have actively preserved the past so that they could understand the new. They have carefully and reverentially preserved, renewed, and renovated their temples and vigorously continued their martial arts, such as *kendō, jūdō,* and *kyūdo,* and traditional arts, such as flower arrangement, tea ceremony and calligraphy. Great numbers of people are still involved in the traditional folk and fine arts, including ceramics, painting, *Yamato-e*, weaving and papermaking, which help to enhance their lives.

At the same time, they make constant efforts to enhance their lives in a modern setting as new and foreign elements continue to change their culture. For example, the Japanese have always revered nature and are quicker than most other people to notice such phenomena as global warming and try to take preventative measures. At the present time, the Japanese are leading the world in the use of solar energy.

The Japanese have looked at their history and realized that much of their social and political policies were too narrowly centered and are now are consciously trying to become more involved in international affairs. To this end, they are also trying to improve their generally negative images and much of their current effort is to be more active in presenting the more positive components in their culture. The *Issei* have actively used their past to enhance their lives in an advanced Western country. When they came to the United States they found a culture so modern and different that they reevaluated their traditional values yet found them to be relevant to the new society because they helped them fulfill the American Dream.

## Goal Orientation

In his book, "A New Look at Modern History", Professor Edwin Reischauer listed the existence of the idea of goal orientation as one of the factors in Japan's rapid Westernization. To Reischauer, "goal orientation means that one seeks the accomplishment of specific objectives as the highest ideal." This outlook is in contrast to "status orientation" which he describes as follows, "Status orientation means that one seeks recognition, not for what one has accomplished substantively, but through one's official status in society, such as high public office or an honorable and respected social position.  Although all societies contain elements of both orientations, there do exist differences of emphasis between different societies."[15]  Thus, when the Western nations began to exploit the Japanese, the Japanese goal was to modernize (Westernize) their country and free themselves from Western intrusion and influence.

The *Issei* immigrants, as noted throughout this book, were also highly goal oriented, their goal being to try to help the children become productive citizens by working and studying hard.  "Study and work hard.  Don't lose to the white folks," were the oft repeated encouragement that the *Nisei* children heard from their parents.  The *Issei* also had to meet more immediate challenges, such as racism, depression, and war, to make certain that their children would be able to achieve their goals.  They constantly repeated that "This is life and we can't give in or give up.  We must persevere!"  How many times did the *Nisei* hear parents say, "Endure (*gaman seyo*)," or "persevere (*shinbo seyo*)"?

## Working Together

The Japanese often say the world is interdependent that people need to support others and be supported by others (*mochitsu motaretsu*).  They feel that people need to work together harmoniously if they expect not only to survive but to succeed in life.  The *Issei* understood this concept most vividly when they faced hostility and discrimination from the very first moment they arrived in the United States.  Thus, they banded together to create a strong Japanese community which would serve to  provide a sense of security against the onslaught of unfriendly and hostile people who seemed to oppose their effort to secure their "piece of the American Pie."  The community also played a major part in reinforcing their most important goal of ensuring their children's future. It was a major aspect of living for "*kodomo no tame ni.*" The community reinforced the values taught at home and helped keep their children from straying too far from these values. The Japanese Language Schools, *kenjinkais*, and other organizations all strengthened the *Nikkei* community.

As mentioned earlier, the family members worked harmoniously to help the family survive and flourish, particularly after most of them were released from the concentration camp and had to start from scratch. Because education was considered vital to secure a better future most families worked together, so at least one person from the family would be able to continue his/her education beyond high school. Often, the "brightest" in the family were selected to go on as the family would struggle to make sure that would happen. When the family's financial status was more stable, the parents made every effort to send other children to attain education beyond high school.

Another interesting aspect of the Japanese group orientation is the sense of "two - way" loyalty. This notion is exemplified by the Japanese company which makes a strong effort to ensure the employee's economic security by providing lifetime employment and reasonable worker's benefit including retirement income. Of course, much has changed recently as the Japanese companies have begun to emulate the Western way more rigorously and follow the "bottom line" approach. In the case of the *Nikkei* family, the children almost always look after the welfare of their parents at home after their retirement. However, as the economic situation improves with each generation, more and more parents are able to care for themselves, or are sent to retirement homes for better care.

# Part V
## Misunderstanding Stereotypes

The cultural traits briefly described here have generated false images of the Japanese and the *Nikkei*. Stereotypes are formed when people from different cultures meet for the first time. Usually these images are accepted by succeeding generations without much thought as to how accurate they are. One of the strongest images many Americans have of the Japanese is that they are the "students" and the Westerners, particularly the Americans, are the "teachers." It is easy to come to this conclusion because the Americans did open Japan's door in the 1850's and introduced modern civilization to the Japanese. The corollary image is that the Americans have always been "friend" and "benefactors" to the Japanese while the Japanese were the "recipients" and "takers" of American kindness. Another reason to reinforce these images is the fact that the Japanese immigrated to America and generally succeeded in sharing the abundance of America. Many Americans also believe that they generously helped Japan to recover from the devastating losses of the Second World War. The Japanese image as "takers" changed to "ungrateful takers" when the Japanese startled the world with their relative quick economic recovery, but many Americans felt that the Japanese were taking unfair advantage of the trade between the two countries.[16]

On a personal level, many Americans formed a very negative image when they first met the *Issei* immigrants. Most were poor laborers and their life style was so different from the Americans, in general, that they began to characterize the *Issei* as dirty, smelly, ignorant heathens. Many *Issei* expressed their anger and said, "Those Americans think that they are so great (*erai*) and we are so ignorant (*orokamon*). And they always say that we are dirty (*kitanai, fuketsu*) and smell a lot (*totemo kusai*). They act like they aren't dirty or smell themselves. At least we take bath every night, but the *hakujin* take a bath once a week.[17] They say we are savages (*yabanjin*) because we eat raw fish and other smelly food. That's because they don't know the taste of *sashimi* or *takuan* (pickled radish) so we can say that they are the *bakamon* (stupid fool)." Although these retorts were said often, most of the *Issei* felt grateful to be in America and to be able to share in the American Dream and, as mentioned earlier, the parents reminded their *Nisei* children that they are Americans and they owe loyalty to this country.

Another common stereotype of the Japanese was that they were "copycats" devoid of any creativity or originality. Many Americans knew that the Japanese borrowed Confucian, Buddhist, Shinto, and Christian ideas but could not understand how individuals could accept a combination of these religions without being hypocritical or contradictory. To many Americans it was inconceivable that anyone could borrow good and positive points of each of the different religions. Many people do not know that the Japanese have always been religiously tolerant and never fought large scale religious wars or branded other faiths as "false" or "evil." They felt that the Japanese were heathens who lacked true faith and integrity. Thus, from the American perspective, *Issei* were "inassimilable" and not fit to be Americans.

## Integrating American Ideals and Japanese Values

In 1984, President Reagan made a speech praising the Asian Americans, including the Japanese Americans, for helping to preserve the American Dream[18] by "living up to the bedrock values of America – the principles of the sacred worth of human life, religious faith, community spirit, and the responsibility of parents and schools to be teachers of tolerance, hard work, fiscal responsibility, cooperation and love." It was an apt acknowledgement of the *Nisei*, who contributed to the society in general, to their communities in particular, and earned a great deal of respect from the general public.

However, despite the praise they belatedly received from many segments of the American public, the *Nikkei* people lacked positive feelings about themselves. Many *Nisei* tended to blame the "Japanese" training they received from their parents for the negative feelings they had about themselves. The defeat of Japan convinced many *Nisei* to feel, perhaps unconsciously and unwittingly, that their parents' way of thinking and doing was wrong and they continued to reject much of their parents' motives and values.

Even before the war, and especially after war, many *Nisei* community leaders publicly rejected Japanese things and espoused 110 percent Americanism. In a practical sense, many *Nisei* accepted American culture completely and criticized those people who retained anything of Japanese culture as old fashioned and out of step with the rest of America. In this kind of an atmosphere, it was no surprise that many of the *Issei* parents began to lose credibility with their children.

Thus, many *Nisei*, as well as other people, began to assume that their success was a result of adopting the American way of life and incorporating mainstream American values. This belief took root in spite of the fact that many social scientists who attributed the success of the Japanese Americans to the values which were taught to them by their *Issei* parents. President Reagan's well intentioned assertion was misleading and his speech was another instance of perceiving Japanese as "good students" learning from the *hakujins*. Let us take a closer look the values which he praised.

## Sacred Worth of Human Life

We all know about the American Constitution which centers around the concept of individual freedom and rights for all, reflecting our belief in the sacred worth of the individual. But how many of us know about the first Japanese Constitution in the 7th Century known as the 17 Article Constitution which was based on Buddhist ideas? The author of this important document, Prince Shōtoku, was the first ruler to recognize the worth of the common people, and much of the constitution emphasized the human and compassionate treatment of the common people. Of course, the rights of the individual were not written out explicitly and assertively as in the U.S. Constitution; nevertheless, the first Japanese Constitution clearly recognized the worth of the individual.

Although our American Constitution guaranteed in writing certain rights to individuals, the *Issei* and the *Nisei* were frequently denied the respect that the Constitution promised. But the *Issei* transcended America's demeaning two-class system with their strong sense of identity and unyielding spiritual strength. They did so by raising the self esteem of *Nikkei* individuals and proving that Asians and non-Christians no longer needed to be ashamed to be Buddhist, Confucian, or Shinto. They also demonstrated that a *Nikkei* who knew how to speak, read, and write the Japanese language was no less of an American. Ironically, the

*Nisei* with the greatest amount of self esteem were those who were most Anglicized.

By tradition and moral training, Japanese immigrants, like their ancestors in Japan, emphasized the sacred worth of all living beings, and in their personal lives, they were very careful to express their gratitude to all living things. Long before American politicians and activists began speaking out for environmental protection, the *Issei*, with their sense of *mottainai*, taught frugality, cautioned against excessive luxury, and practiced conservation of valuable natural resources. The *Issei* recognized the limitations of the planet and knew that rampant material acquisition could only deprive others, including the coming generations, of the ever decreasing natural resources. Most Japanese led a spartan life trying to teach that beauty comes from simplicity and frugality. The *Issei* were extraordinary models of people observing the sacred worth of all living beings.

## Religious Faith

The Japanese expression of religious faith is quite different from that of Westerners. Japanese have an eclectic attitude toward religion which allows them to combine their traditional views with different ones, so, as mentioned previously, a Japanese person can practice Buddhist, Confucian, and Christian customs at the same time. However, no matter how much they incorporated different religious views, the Japanese retained the basic concepts of gratitude, compassion, and harmony. This kind of syncretic outlook is considered contradictory and paradoxical to many Westerners; as a result, some thought that the Japanese were heathens who lacked true faith. Even in today's America, there is a strong core of people who believe that any deviation from their notion of a monotheistic Christian God is heretical, and they continue to look at other religions with suspicion, disdain, and even hatred.

## Community Spirit And Cooperation

The Japanese had always emphasized strong and unified community spirit. They had always believed that the family and community were the two most important parts of their society and always been an important value that the Japanese emphasized through much of her history. However, many Americans believed that the Japanese emphasized community spirit to the detriment of the interest and needs of individuals. They never understood that the *Issei* created their communities to protect the interests and needs of individuals, particularly their children's and their families. Certainly, at this time, the many diverse communities in the U.S. are not unified or very harmonious. The Japanese American communities can provide valuable lessons and inspirations for many communities to emulate and to learn.

How could the *Issei* build such a strong and stable community without the spirit of cooperation among the people? When the *Issei* emphasized the spirit of cooperation and concord, they were criticized for sacrificing the needs of the individual. But today, our society has focused so much on individualism that we have a difficult time engendering a spirit of cooperation even in sports, for example, where teamwork and cooperation is so vital.

## Tolerance

The Japanese had accepted and adapted foreign points of view from the earliest time in their history. Because of this flexible and tolerant attitude, the *Issei* and their children were able to acculturate quickly to American customs and beliefs.  Again, so adept and tolerant were the Japanese that they were accused of being copy cats and devoid of original thought.  Although as Americans, we have preached tolerance in our society for a long, long time, we still have a difficult time respecting differences in religion, birth country, gender, and sexuality.  Those differences have been the cause of much conflict within our society.

## Fiscal Responsibility

Over the years, according to the culture of the decades, there were many Americans who talked about financial responsibility but failed to exhibit real fiscal responsibility. Currently, many Americans have huge debt from using their credit cards, and an excessive number of people  have declared personal bankruptcy.  In contrast, when the *Issei* came to America, a land of plenty, they were willing to work hard in order to save enough money to return home in glory.  When circumstances did not allow this to happen, they continued to work, work, work and save, save, save as they had in Japan until they reached their economic goal.  Again and again, the *Issei* impressed upon their *Nisei* children  the value of *mottainai* and living a life of frugality.

## Responsibility of the Parents

Through the centuries, public figures in America have often promoted the importance of parents imparting to children certain basic values of America, values such as hard work, tolerance, education, and honesty.  For most *Issei*, such reminders were entirely unnecessary.   The *Issei* themselves learned from their parents and ancestors happened to be congruent with these  American values.

In short, when President Reagan praised the Japanese

Americans for living up to the bedrock values of America, he failed to recognize: (1) that the bedrock values he spoke of were congruent with the inherent *Issei* values; and (2) that they had instilled these beliefs in their children from their early childhood and they were already part of their personality and character. Unfortunately, many *Nisei*, were also unaware of the values inculcated by their parents nor the depth and relevance of their parents' teachings.

# Conclusion

What relevance can the *Issei* legacy have in our society today? Many Americans have doubts about the ability of our institutions and our elected officials to unify our society and lessen the deepening divide between the rich and the powerless which include the poor, the old, and the young. We also are concerned about crime and the moral decline in their society, i.e., the seeming loss of policies emphasizing the public good rather than the encouragement of personal and corporate aggrandizement. There is increasing worry about the singular interest in the pursuit of personal happiness with little concern about diminishing natural resources. The inability of too many of our citizens to get beyond their self concern and self interest seems to be tearing down much that is right about our society.

Slowly, a number of people are beginning to see that our lives require more than material possessions; we are considering the possibility of reforming some aspects of our overall perspectives and assumptions and to reassert the promise of America. A look backwards makes it clear that the ideas and values of those courageous Japanese immigrants, who so often started their lives in America at the lowest possible social scale, holds valuable and valid insights for American society today even in light of the magnitude of today's social problems.

The *Issei* were deeply aware of the interdependent nature of the world and believed that individuals should acknowledge and express appreciation to all beings rather than exploit nature solely for the immediate benefit of human beings. By example, they tried to teach that nature and its limited resources needed to be conserved for the sake of all people for all time. Even as they achieved a certain amount of economic security, most *Issei* never lapsed into a life of luxury or the pursuit of more material acquisitions. Many never changed their simple and frugal ways.

The *Issei* also believed that this sense of appreciation should be extended to all who contributed to the growth and well being of the individual. Thus, they were constantly reminded to cooperate with others and work together in harmony and peace. *Issei* parents certainly did not encourage the very American notion that rugged individualism was the key to an individual's accomplishments. However, they believed very strongly that the individual had the responsibility to make the supreme effort to work and study hard and to persevere over difficulties and obstacles. Still, they were taught never to forget the collective efforts of family, relatives, friends, and countless numbers of invisible helpers. Thus, it was their responsibility to work for the welfare of all beings, the society and the world.

*Issei* parents also tried to engender a spirit of tolerance, nurturing a strong religious faith to bring coherence to the society rather than the separation of all people through dogma, tyranny, ignorance, and apathy. These views and ideas were not an idle list of ideals but were borne out of living through great difficulties and transcending them. All of these ideas crystallized in the process of bringing up their children who went on to become one of the greatest generations in history.

The *Issei* legacy did not end with their *Nisei* children;

their spirit has been continued *actively* in the local temples and churches and in other institutions in the *Nikkei* community. Year after year, the *Nikkei* communities continue to carry out the cultural rituals. For example, the community still celebrates and thanks its elders, honors their children, and remembers to serve the less fortunate members of the community. The *Nikkei* communities have extended their services to non-*Nikkei* people as well. Therefore the possibility of incorporating the ways of the *Issei* to restore the noble task of individuals working together for the common good and fulfilling the American Promise more fully and meaningfully is realistic. It is certainly well worth our time to explore such a possibility. If we could have asked the *Issei* of such possibility, they would have said, "Nobody would even think of such an incredible (*daisoreta*) idea."

The *Issei* had no speeches given on their behalf, certainly no wall of honor built for them, and the *Issei* did not find it necessary to have others recognize their achievements because they knew themselves what they accomplished and they were content in the knowledge that they had, indeed, done the best for the sake of their children (*kodomo no tame ni*). Most of them simply stated, "*atarimae no koto o atarimae ni shita dake desuyo.*" (I just did the most natural thing in the most natural way.) And, almost all of the *Issei* I had met, when asked, "How do you feel about your life?" answered, "I am content. I've had much hardship but because of all the help I received from others, I am living happily and gratefully."

# Footnotes

[1] *Sei* means generation. Then the numbers from one are added to the term generation. Thus, the first generation immigrants from Japan are called *Issei*. The children of the *Issei* are called *Nisei*.

[2] At first, when the Japanese and the Japanese Americans were removed to the concentration camps, they were euphemistically called relocation camps /centers. Even today, many people feel uncomfortable with the term concentration camp and continue to use the term relocation camp/ center.

[3] Some people feel that the body odor of a person is highly influenced by the food one eats. For example, the Japanese think that their odor is influenced by *shōyu* (soy sauce), *miso* (soy paste), fish sauce, and *takuan* (pickled radish). To many Japanese, Americans smell of dairy products and meat.

[4] An excellent account of this incident and the early history of the *Issei* can be found in Ronald Takaki's *Strangers From a Different Shore: A History of Asian Americans,* Penguin Books, New York, New York, 1989.

[5] At first, the Japanese immigrants could not purchase any land, but a few *Issei* had their trusted Caucasian friends buy the land in their names. Later, when the *Issei* had children, they purchased the land under their names because they were American citizens by birth and therefore legally able to buy land.

[6] Many *Nisei* also were hired because they were not able to find employment elsewhere.

[7] *Kibei* is a term used for children of the *Issei* who were sent to Japan for various reasons and who returned to the United States. Understandably, they were imbued with varying degrees of Japanese cultural values. *Ki* is a term meaning return and *bei* means America. It is a contraction of the term *Beikoku* (America.)

[8] Many Japanese proverbs translated into English can be found in books such as David Galef's *Even Monkeys Fall From Trees,* and *Even a Stone Buddha Can Talk,* both books published by Tuttle Publishing, Tokyo, 1987 and 2000, and Guy A. Zona's *Even Withered Trees Give Prosperity to the Mountain,* Touchstone, Rockefeller Center, Simon and Shuster Inc., 1996.

[9] For those people who can read Japanese, a detailed history of the Japanese Language School is well documented in the book, *Zaibei Nihonjin-shi. The History of the Japanese Living in the United States,* Association of Japanese Living in the United States, San Francisco, California, 1941.

[10] Japanese felt that the *Meiji* Period was a revolutionary change to a modern nation and the people born in that era were extremely proud to be part of the great transformation.

[11] Kazuko Higaki, *Ayumi,* Nihon Tosha, Tokyo, Japan, 1990.

[12] Historically, the Japanese considered the *Eta* as outcasts because they did work considered to be "impure" such as slaughtering animals and working on leather goods. To marry an *Eta* was unthinkable by the Japanese, and when the *Issei* came to America, they continued the discrimination.

Whenever the matter of marriage came up regarding their children, the parents would make a thorough background check to make sure that the prospective marriage partner was not an *Eta*. The *Issei* also considered the Koreans and the Okinawans to be undesirable people and treated them as unequals.

[13] The new "upper class" consisted of those *Issei* who had achieved economic success and those who became community leaders even though they might not have been affluent. Also considered "higher" than most, were *Issei* who had a college education or high school education. This class distinction was not as clearly defined or rigidly observed as the traditional class system in Japan.

[14] Three of the more interesting studies on Japanese cultural values are: Eiichiro, Ishida, *Tōzaishō, East West Selections,* Chikuma Shobo, Tokyo, 1967, (in Japanese); Charles A. Moore, Ed., *The Japanese Mind: Essentials of Japanese Philososphy and Culture,* East West Center Press, University of Hawaii Press, Honlolulu, 1967; and Daniel Okimoto and Thomas Rohlen, Ed., *Inside the Japanese System: Readings on Contemporary Society and Political Economy,* Stanford Universisty Press, Stanford, California, 1988.

[15] In 1965, Edwin Reischauer, a noted scholar of Japanese history and U.S. Ambassador, to Japan, published an interesting tract, *A New Look at Modern History,* Hara Shobo, Tokyo 1964, on the two different responses of China and Japan to the Western intrusion into their countries.

[16] A more detailed description of the "student - teacher" image of the Japanese and the Americans was discussed in my article, *"Japanese – American  History Given Away"* in

the *California Council for the Social Studies Review, 1970-1971.*

[17] In the 1930's, I remember two of my public school teachers telling the class that taking a bath every night as the Japanese did was not good because it would make the skin too dry. They said that the American "Saturday Night Bath/Shower" was the best. One of the teachers further stated that the Japanese nightly bath custom was foolish.

[18] The discussion of President Reagan's speech and the image of Asian Americans, including the Japanese Americans, as the model minority can be found in previously cited work of Ronald Takaki's *Strangers From a Different Shore.*

# Recommended Readings

Davies, Roger J., and Osamu Ikeno, ed., *The Japanese Mind: Understanding Contemporary Japanese Culture,*Tuttle Publishing, Tokyo, 2002.

Gordon, Milton M., *Assimilation in American Life: The Role of Race, Religion, and National Origins*, Oxford University Press, 1964.

Ichioka, Yuji, *The Issei,* the Free Press, a Division of Macmillan, Inc., 1988.

Kitano, Harry, *Japanese Americans: The Evolution of a Subculture*, Prentice-Hall, Inc., Englewood Cliffs, New Jersey, 1969.

Kiyama, Henry (Yoshitaka), *The Four Immigrants Manga: A Japanese Experience in San Francisco, 1904 - 1924*, translated with an introduction and notes by Frederik L. Schodt, Stone Bridge Press, Berkeley, California, 2005.

Lebra, Takie Sugiyama, *Japanese Patterns of Behavior*, University of Hawaii Press, Honolulu, 1976.

Moore, Charles, Ed., *The Japanese Mind*, East West Center Press, University of Hawaii, Honolulu, 1967.

Okimoto, Daniel, and Thomas Rohlen, ed., *Inside the Japanese System, Readings on Contemporary Society and Political Economy*, Stanford University Press, Stanford, California, 1988.

Reischauer, Edwin O., *A New Look at Modern History*, Hara Shobo, Tokyo, 1964.

# Recommended Readings

Sarasohn, Eileen Sunada, ed. *Issei Women: Echoes From Another Frontier*, Pacific Books, Publishers, Palo Alto, California, 1998.

Sarasohn, Eileen Sunada, ed, *The Issei, Portrait of a Pioneer*, Pacific Books, Publishers, Palo Alto, California, l983.

## Books in Japanese

Asano Shichinosuke, *Zaibei Yonjyunen, Watashi no Kiroku* 在 米四十年 私の記録 (*Living in America Forty Years, My Chronicle*), Yuuki Shobo, Tokyo, 1962.

East Bay Japanese for Action, translated and ed., *Watashita-chi no Kiroku (Our Recollections)* 私達の記録., Tokyo Art Printing Company, Ltd., 1986.

Higaki, Kazuko, translated by Tauchi Aiko, *Ayumi (Steps)*.歩み, Nihon Tosha, Inc., Tokyo, 1976.

Ishida, Eiichiro, *Tozaishō* 東西抄, *(East West Selections)* Chikuma Shobo, Tokyo, 1967.

Tana, Daishō and Tana, Tomoe, Yoku*ryushō Nikki (Concentration Camp Diary)* 抑留所日記, 3 volumes, Yamabiko, Busshorin, Tokyo, 1976.

Zaibei Nipponjin Kai, ed., *Zaibei Nipponjin Shi (History of Japanese Living in America)*, Kyodo Insatsu Kabushiki Kaisha, Tokyo, 1940.

## Japanese - English Glossary

| | |
|---|---|
| Akirameru 諦める | Accept the situation; be resign |
| Arigatō 有難う | Thanks |
| Baishakunin 媒酌人 | Matchmaker |
| Baka(na) 馬鹿な | Foolish; stupid |
| Bōnenkai 忘年会 | Year end party |
| Bonsai 盆栽 | Dwarfed tree |
| Chambara (movie) ちゃんばら | Sword fighting samurai movie |
| Chonmage ちょんまげ | Top knot hairstyle |
| Chūsei 忠誠 | Loyalty |
| Daiji 大事 | Important |
| Dekiru dake 出来るだけ | As much as one can |
| Doryoku 努力 | Effort; exert |
| Furisode 振り袖 | Long sleeved kimono |
| Gaman 我慢 | Be patient; bear; endure |
| Giri 義理 | Obligation |
| Go 碁 | Japanese board game |
| Gochisō 御馳走 | Delicious meal; treat |
| Gochisōsama ご馳走様 | Word of thanks for a nice meal |
| Gohan ご飯 | Cooked rice |
| Haiku 俳句 | Japanese poem of 17 syllables |
| Hakujin 白人 | White person |
| Hanafuda はなふだ | Japanese card game |
| Heimin へいみん | Common people |
| Hito 人 | Person |
| Hōgen 方言 | Regional dialect |
| Ichiban 一番 | The best; number one |
| Ika いか | Cuttlefish; squid |
| Ikebana 生花 | Art of flower arrangement |

| | |
|---|---|
| Inarizushi 稲荷寿司 | Boiled vinegared rice in fried bean curd |
| Inochi 命 | Life |
| Ishi 石 | Stone; rock |
| Issei 一世 | First generation of Japanese immigrants |
| Isshiki 一式 | Formal part of ceremony |
| Itadakimasu 頂きます | Saying thanks before meals |
| Jinsei 人生 | Life |
| Kansha 感謝 | Gratitude; thanks |
| Karuta カルタ | Japanese card game |
| Kazunoko 数の子 | Herring roe |
| Kei 敬 | Respect |
| Keigo 敬語 | Respectful language |
| Keirōkai 敬老会 | Respect the elders party |
| Kenbu 剣舞 | Japanese sword dance |
| Kenjinkai 県人会 | Association of people from the same prefecture |
| Kenkō 健康 | Health; fitness |
| Kenson 謙遜 | Modesty; humility |
| Ketō 毛唐 | Hairy barbarian |
| Kibei 帰米 | Japanese Americans who were sent to Japan and then returned to the United States |
| Kombu 昆布 | Kelp |
| Koto 事 | A matter |
| Kotowaza 諺 | Proverb; maxim |
| Kurō 苦労 | Hardship; suffering |
| Kuromame 黒豆 | Black soybean |
| Kuyokuyo くよくよ | Overly worry or fret about |
| Kyōiku 教育 | Education |
| Makeru 負ける | Lose |

| | |
|---|---|
| Makizushi 巻き寿司 | Rolled sushi |
| Mi 身 | Person; body |
| Miai 見合い | Marriage meeting |
| Mikan みかん | Tangerine |
| Minna 皆 | Everyone, everything |
| Mochi 餅 | Rice cake |
| Mokuteki 目的 | Purpose; goal |
| Mono 物 | A thing; matter; goods |
| Mottainai 勿体無い | Too valuable to waste |
| Nihongo 日本語 | Japanese language |
| Nihonmachi 日本町 | Japantown |
| Nikkei 日系 | Descendents of Japanese heritage |
| Nisei 二世 | Second generation |
| Nishiki o kazaru 錦を飾る | To display in brocade "Return home covered in glory" |
| Obentō 御弁当 | Boxed lunch |
| *Obon* お盆 | Lantern festival; festival of the dead. |
| Okage お陰 | Thanks to…; owing to…. |
| Omoiyari おもいやり | Thoughtful; considerate |
| On 恩 | Debt of gratitude |
| Orei お礼 | Thanks; gratitude |
| Orokamon(o) 愚か者 | A foolish, stupid person |
| Oshōgatsu お正月 | The New Year |
| Otagaisama お互い様 | "In the same boat" |
| Otoshidama お年玉 | New Year's gift |
| Oyakōkō 親孝行 | Filial piety |
| Renkon 蓮根 | Lotus root |
| Sado 茶道 | Tea ceremony |
| Sambasan 産婆さん | Midwife |
| San-in 産院 | Maternity hospital |
| Sato imo 里芋 | Taro |

| | |
|---|---|
| Seishinryoku 精神力 | Spiritual power |
| Senryu 川柳 | Seventeen syllable satirical poem |
| Shamisen 三味線 | Three stringed Japanese musical instrument |
| Shashin kekkon 写真結婚 | Picture wedding |
| Shigin 詩吟 | Chanting of a poem |
| Shikata ga nai 仕方がない | Forced or compelled to do, no other option |
| Shimbō 辛抱 | Perseverance |
| Shinenkai 新年会 | A New Year's party |
| Shitsuke 躾 | Child rearing |
| Shizoku 士族 | A descendant of a samurai warrior |
| Shodō 書道 | Calligraphy |
| Shōgi 将棋 | Japanese chess |
| Sumi-e 墨絵 | India-ink drawing |
| Sumō 相撲 | Japanese wrestling |
| Sunao 素直 | Obedient |
| Tai 鯛 | Sea bream |
| Tsuyoi 強い | Strong |
| Utai 謡い | Chanting of a Noh text |
| Utsukushii 美しい | Beautiful |
| Wa 和 | Harmony |
| Yamato 大和 | Old term for Japan |
| Yo 世 | The world |
| Yukata 浴衣 | An informal cotton kimono for summer |
| Yume 夢 | Dream |
| Zeitaku 贅沢 | Luxury |

## Biography of Author

 Tsukasa Matsueda was born in Stockton, California and later moved to San Mateo California. At age 16, he was incarcerated at Stockton Assembly Center, Rohwer, Arkansas, and Tule Lake, California. After his release from the concentration camps, he was drafted into Military Service where he served in the 525th Military Intelligence Unit.

Matsueda received a B.A. from the University of California, Berkeley; a M.A. from the San Francisco State University, and Ed. D. from the University of Massachusetts. He taught 33 years at Sequoia Union High School in Redwood City, CA. Selected as a Fulbright Exchange Teacher to Japan, he taught for two years at the University of Niigata and the attached Junior High School in Niigata City, Japan. Later, he taught Japanese American Ethnic Studies classes at Stanford University and San Jose State University. When he retired from teaching, Matsueda served as a Case Manager for the Japanese speaking clientile at Yu-Ai Kai, the Japanese American Community Senior Service in San Jose for over ten years.

Presently, he is retired and residing with his wife of 50 years, June, in Palo Alto, California. He has a son, Bob, daughter-in-law, Ranko, and grandson, Ken; and a daughter, Julie, son-in-law, Jon, and grandchildren, Mika and Lee.